FORMICA®
& DESIGN

First published in the United States of America in 1991
by Rizzoli International Publications, Inc.
300 Park Avenue South, New York, NY 10010

Library of Congress Cataloging-in-Publications Data

**Formica and design: from the counter top to high art /
Susan Grant Lewin, [editor].**
p. cm.
Includes bibliographical references.
Includes index.
ISBN 0-8478-1334-7
1. Formica Corporation. 2. Laminated plastics.
3. Plastics in interior decoration. 4. United States—
Popular culture—History—20th Century. I. Grant Lewin, Susan.
NK2004.3.F67F67   1991   90-50793
729—dc20   CIP

Pages 1, 2: F-Chips. Photo: Bill Kontzias.

Formica, the Anvil F devise, ColorCore, Surell, The Color Grid,
Design Concepts, Lacque Metallique, and The International
Collection are registered trademarks of Formica Corporation.

FORMICA® & DESIGN

FROM THE COUNTER TOP TO HIGH ART

Editor

Susan Grant Lewin

Introduction by

R. Craig Miller

Essays by

Sarah Bayliss, Sarah Bodine and Micheal Dumas,
Alessandro De Gregori, Barbara Goldstein,
Richard J.S. Gutman, Steven Holt, Karrie Jacobs,
Simon Leung, Jeffrey L. Meikle,
and Marybeth Shaw.

Afterword by

Vincent P. Langone

Design by

Doublespace

RIZZOLI
NEW YORK

To the legacy of the Design Advisory Board and to anyone who has ever become a Formican. To my family: Hal, Adam, Gaby, Jeannie, and my mother.

Susan Grant Lewin

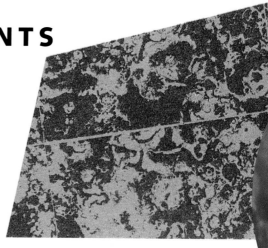

CONTENTS

PREFACE

This book grew out of research originally begun in 1987, just before Formica Corporation's seventy-fifth anniversary. At that time, Formica artifacts and memorabilia of all kinds were solicited by the New York office to help develop a company time line and seventy-fifth-anniversary commemorative calendar. As the old advertisements, company brochures, pamphlets, sample chains, books, and photographs of events and installations poured in from across the country—and from around the world—it became apparent that the variety and interest of these archival materials lent themselves to much more than a time line. The rich collection of information, imagery, and products, which spanned over eighty years, suggested to us a book that would trace American popular culture and taste through the history of Formica laminate.

It may at first seem unlikely that the history of twentieth-century design could be embodied in a material as prosaic as Formica laminate. As it happens, however, a case study of a specific product, design, or company can serve as an index of popular culture and taste, revealing much about the broader evolution of design issues. A product resulting from technological developments that respond to the needs of culture can in turn affect it. The history of Formica laminate encapsulates the changes in vernacular taste, style, consumer habits, and values over the past eighty years.

The structure of this book was suggested by the original source material we collected. A 1988 *New York* magazine article by Kay Larson on Richard Artschwager's one-man show at the Whitney Museum of American Art in New York spawned two chapter ideas: artists' attraction to Formica laminate, an area explored by Sarah Bodine and Michael Dunas in "Plastic Expression," and the seduction of simulation, discussed in Steven Holt's "The Phenomenon of Formica." The company's constantly changing logo and graphic identity provided a history lesson on design in miniature, as Karrie Jacobs reveals in "The Logo." Even the shifting cultural attitudes toward women were expressed through the material, as Sarah H. Bayliss argues in "The Laminate Woman." From the standpoint of industry and corporate culture, the company's history and the history of plastic—topics of chapters by Steven Holt and Jeffrey Meikle, respectively—proved to be examples of great American success stories. Two other chapters in this book trace additional aspects of the product. Marybeth Shaw, who worked in Formica Corporation's New York office, delves into the product's colors and patterns as it responded to shifts in popular taste from the 1930s to current pluralistic design, with styles changing at a merciless pace. The especially colorful decade of the fifties, driven both by the birth of consumerism and the need for conformity, is brought to life by Barbara Goldstein, in "Formica in the Fifties." Sidebars by Richard Gutman and Simon Leung explain why Formica laminate was the perfect material for diners (those "machines for cooking"), and how the material adapted itself to fit gender classifications. Leung further investigates and rediscovers Brooks Stevens, the relatively obscure, but very important designer who coined the term "planned obsolescence." I provide a tour of the

product's more recent developments and incarnations—exhibitions of jewelry, furniture, and conceptual objects, as well as the material's graphic and advertising identities.

A vast amount of work was required to shape a sprawling collection of good information and images into a "good read." Three people, above all, deserve special recognition, and I can't thank them enough. Marybeth Shaw, Simon Leung, and Jo Anne Schlesinger dedicated themselves to the book. Steven Holt was invaluable in helping me to shape the structure of the book and in determining the best authors for the various chapters. And thanks should also be extended to Sarah Bayliss for her imaginative coordination and research.

Also deserving grateful acknowledgments are R. Craig Miller, Dennis Galli, Bob Kilbury, Kris Benson, Bob Whittemore, Joe Cullen, Don Steffan, Evelyn McCarthy, Herm Bass, Alessandro De Gregori, Suzanne Ramljak, Dennis Barrie, David McFadden, Gary Wolf, Brooks Stevens, Albert J. Heeb, Mrs. Carol Willard, Hank Shear, Stuart Faber, Richard Gutman, Beth Gerowitz and Chillingworth/Radding, Michael Beirut, David Sterling, Jane Kosstrin, and Klaus Kempenaars for their innovative and appropriate design, Robert Janjigian for his infinite patience, sense of humor, and sensitivity to the material, Charles Brooks for his absolutely invaluable advice, and, of course, Vince Langone, without whose encouragement and support this book would not have been possible.

Thank you, also, to Frank Gehry, Stanley Tigerman, Robert Venturi, the Vignellis, Emilio Ambasz, and Beverly Russell, long-standing friends who always said, "Yes." And countless others.

Introduced some eighty years ago, Formica laminate continues to be a strong design element today. The product is endlessly transformed—by new colors and patterns, and by new applications that explore the cutting edge of contemporary design as well as an international consumer-based aesthetic. The future of Formica laminate is secure as the material promises to change, develop, and reinvent itself in adaptation to our changing world in the coming century.

Susan Grant Lewin

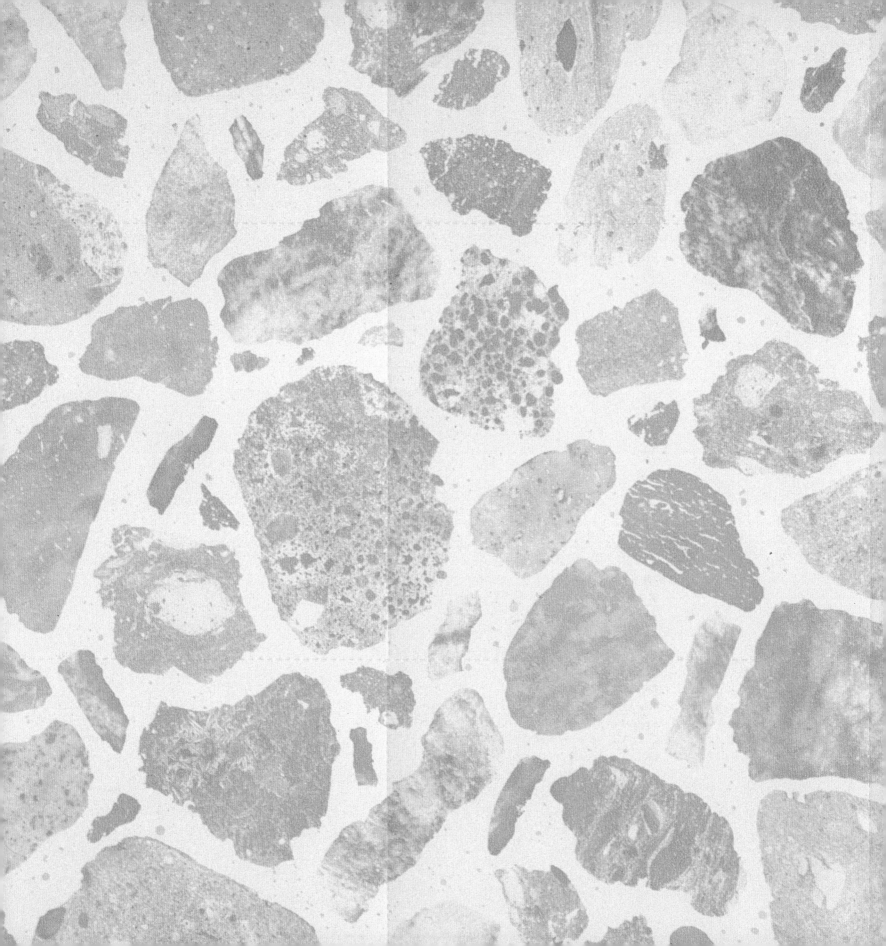

INTRODUCTION

American architecture is the art of covering one thing with another to imitate a third thing, which, if genuine, would not be desirable.

So wrote Leopold Eidletz, a noted New York designer, almost a century ago. Eidletz's comment was decidedly cynical, but he recognized one of the basic conflicts in Modernist design: a concern for architectonic form, function, and materials versus the desire for decorative color, ornament, pattern, and, especially, *faux* finishes. In the twentieth century, perhaps no industrial product has been such an integral part of this continuing debate as Formica laminate. This book traces its evolution as a material and its pervasive— though in many ways unrecognized—effect on American society.

Twentieth-century industrial design has been shaped largely by three materials: tubular steel, molded plywood, and polymer substances, popularly known as plastics. The first two were developed in Europe between the world wars and entered the design field through the Modernist avant-garde. Tubular steel had its greatest impact on the furniture industry; the use of light, resilient frames radically altered design in the 1920s and was crucial to the development of cantilevered chairs. Plywood, of course, had been used throughout much of the nineteenth century as a secondary sheeting material and as an exposed surface in innovative Victorian furniture. It was not until the 1930s, however, that its architectonic qualities—its ability to be bent and molded—were fully exploited by the Modernists in a wide variety of products.

The development of plastics, on the other hand, has largely occurred in America as part of the mass culture of the post–World War II period. As with plywood, the history of plastics began in the nineteenth century. Synthetic substances — such as celluloid and casein — were first created as cheaper substitutes for other materials. In 1907 a major technological breakthrough occurred with the creation of Bakelite, the first completely synthetic resin, and this was followed six years later by another laminated sheeting material, Formica brand laminate. During the twenties and thirties, product research advanced at a rapid pace, but it was not until the postwar period that plastics really became a part of our daily lives. Examples from the 1940s and 1950s include fiber-glass shells, followed in the 1960s by polyurethane foam for upholstery and rigid polypropylene for injection-

It is worth asking why Formica laminate has been so attractive to the building industry. Perhaps the answer lies in its inherent simplicity. Formica laminate is a planar sheeting material, although, unlike plywood, it cannot be molded into a third dimension. It requires only elementary handcraftsmanship and may be attached to any secondary substance by straightforward cold-bonding (i.e., glues, rivets, etc.). As a mass-produced product, Formica laminate is durable, inexpensive, and can be made or cut to just about any dimension. The chameleon-like surface of Formica laminate is probably what has assured its success, however, since it can be made in virtually any color or *faux* pattern, including wood, stone, and textile. With its inherent black edge, Formica laminate remained visually a two-dimensional material until 1982, when the introduction of ColorCore® surfacing material made it possible to achieve volumetric as well as intaglio or cameo effects.

molded furniture, not to mention such ubiquitous sealants as polyurethane coatings and plastic wraps.

Formica laminate played a central role in this progressive plasticization of our society. It was used in the second decade of the century as an insulating material for industrial products, but by the 1920s, it began to appear as a surfacing material, although it was not widely used in the design world. Dramatic improvements in its cost and color palette followed quickly, and with the postwar building boom Formica laminate swept through American interiors from the private bathroom to the corporate boardroom. As Formica Corporation expanded, the product began to be consumed on a global scale.

A great deal of attention has been given in this book to the impact of Formica laminate on American culture over the last eight decades. One critical factor in its success has been advertising. Before World War II, the primary market for Formica laminates comprised industrial manufacturers, but after the war they were promoted for the average consumer. Design firms, such as that of Raymond Loewy, were hired in the 1950s to suggest the most appealing colors and patterns; at the same time, a heavy emphasis was placed on cleanliness, efficiency, and femininity in selling the product to American housewives. This was a remarkably successful marketing strategy for almost a quarter of a century, but in the

1970s the company sought a new direction by associating Formica laminate with the growing design consciousness. A design advisory committee was selected to guide the product line, and in the next decade three influential exhibitions were organized by Formica Corporation for the international promotion of the company.

Indeed, one must be wary not to underestimate the enormous power of business and advertising in shaping our concepts of design and society itself. In a relatively short period, Formica laminate became the quintessential American vernacular material. There is perhaps an irony in that at a time when objects made of Formica laminate are at long last entering American museums as works of art: These cultural institutions have begun to package the applied fine arts as a commodity for the same general public.

R. Craig Miller

Steven Holt

THE FORMICA
HISTORY:
IT ISN'T WHAT YOU THINK

Chapter 1

1 | 1

Karrie Jacobs

THE LOGO

23

A nyone who has only a surface acquaintance with Formica brand laminate is likely to believe that it was invented in the 1950s as part of that era's building boom. Or, if not then, perhaps during World War II, as some happy accident of military technology, just as Teflon emerged a few decades later out of the aerospace

program. But the story of Formica laminate isn't what you think. It goes much further back, dating to the dawn of Modernism and to the beginning of what might be called The Plastic Century.

To put things in perspective, Formica laminate was first manufactured in 1913, the same year that Camel cigarettes appeared on the market; the same year that the Lincoln Highway (the first United States coast-to-coast route) was begun; the same year that the legendary Armory Show in New York introduced Americans to the wiles of avant-garde European art. In the second decade of the century, a sense of

1-1
The founders of Formica Corporation, Daniel J. O'Conor (left) and Herbert Faber.

1-2
In front of the Cincinnati factory, ca. 1930.

1-3
The Formica factory in the 1930s.

1-4
The resin plant at the Formica Company's Evendale plant, ca. 1954. Structures such as this resin plant were part of the 1950s' attempt to gain greater control of raw materials.

expectancy and urgency was in the air. This was the spirit that would fully blossom a decade later into the radicalism of Modernist design, and it was the same spirit that created a fertile business climate in industrially inspired cities like Pittsburgh.

Turn-of-the-century Pittsburgh, home to many companies, including Westinghouse Electric and Manufacturing Company, was a "happening place"; the place currently referred to as the Rust Belt was then the shining anchor of a changing nation. The Formica story begins with two young engineers named Herbert A. Faber and Daniel J. O'Conor who found the Pittsburgh/Westinghouse axis irresistible. Faber and O'Conor, not long out of the University of Cincinnati and St. Francis Xavier College of New York, respectively, met in 1907 while both were in their first year of working at Westinghouse. They became fast friends and knew that they were at the center of something good.

Legend has it that at this time Faber and O'Conor met regularly on weekends to discuss what they called their "Vision,"[1] an early, personalized version of The American Dream. It constituted a search for a material that would substantially change their lives and, just maybe, other people's lives, too. Based on the writings of such college-boy luminaries of the times as Thomas Carlyle and Pliny the Elder, their work ethic held that hard work was noble and that the impossible often only looked that way until it was realized. Faber and O'Conor were driven, and they felt the powerful forces of industry sweeping through America. By 1909, with the depression over, the push of new technology swept back with a rush; in 1911 O'Conor was head of the process section in the research engineering department.

1 | 5

In the technical literature of this time, the name of Dr. Leo H. Baekeland comes up repeatedly. Considered the father of modern plastic, Baekeland began to manufacture Bakelite resin (the first totally synthetic plastic) in Yonkers, New York, in 1907. By April of 1910, Baekeland—considered to be a genius in the league of Thomas Edison or Ben Franklin—had been granted seven laminate-based patents.

At Westinghouse, the production of phenolic laminates began in 1910 when heavy canvas was impregnated with Bakelite. O'Conor produced the first laminate sheet by winding and coating paper on a mandrel, slitting the resulting uncured tube, and flattening it by putting it in a press; the patent was applied for on February 1, 1913, and was assigned to Westinghouse (as was company policy, for one dollar). The patent was not issued, however, until November 12, 1918 (because of a government delay in granting it).

In 1913 Faber, by now manager of the insulating materials sales section, knew he had an important new material. Along with

Formica laminate objects, ca. 1930.
Early applications of Formica laminate were mostly industrial.

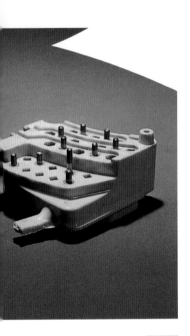

O'Conor, Faber left Westinghouse when the two realized that the company wasn't doing much with its new technology. Like entrepreneurs everywhere, they saw new possibilities on the horizon, and they moved toward it. The "Vision" was starting to seem palpable.

What they needed now was capital. Faber went back home to Cincinnati (a thriving industrial city, where Proctor & Gamble was in the process of laying down roots) and prowled the financial marts while O'Conor went to roam the corridors of Wall Street. Faber found a partner who would risk capital without demanding majority control: J. G. Tomlin, a lawyer and banker from Walton, Kentucky, who anted up $7,500 for a one-third stake in the newly formed Formica Company of Cincinnati.

The product name "Formica," coined by Faber, was appropriate. It indicated that this new plastic material replaced mica, a mineral perfect for insulation but increasingly rare and expensive. Formica laminate, as a material, offered mica's electrical insulating ability but provided greater versatility in application. It should be remembered that early Formica laminate was dark in color, homogeneous, and without a surface layer; indeed, the Formica laminate of the first fifteen years bore little resemblance to the latter-day laminate we know.

After renting two floors at the northeast corner of Second and Main streets for sixty dollars a month, the company's entire equipment list consisted of a 35-horsepower boiler, a small gas stove, and a couple of tables. On May 2, 1913, the company officially opened its doors without presses, treaters, or machine tools of any kind, and, suffice it to say, no

bands, floodlights, or flowers—just Faber and O'Conor, wearing overalls and trying to figure a way to fill their first order for commutator V-rings from the Chalmers Motor Company.

During that first year, the Formica Company led a hand-to-mouth existence. Machines were pushed past their tolerance point, broken, and then jerry-rigged to get an order out. Nonetheless, industry responded well to the Cincinnati upstarts. Ideal Electric (which was later to become Delco Electronics) and Bell Electric Motor both placed orders, driven by the craze for electric starters on automobiles (which required thousands of insulating parts).

Faber and O'Conor went back to Tomlin in August with a simple request: "Give us more money." Tomlin brought in two other partners—banker David Wallace and lawyer John L. Vest—and together they added another $1,100 to Formica's coffers. By September there were eighteen employees, and on October 15, the company was incorporated as The Formica Insulation Company, with Faber as president and treasurer and O'Conor as vice-president and secretary (a situation

that remained unchanged until 1935), six hundred shares were issued at twenty-five dollars each.

In that first year, the company produced only rings and tubes, but by July 4, 1914, the company had obtained a press to produce flat sheets. Formica made laminate only when it had an order, got its resin from the Bakelite Company, and very often sold its finished laminate back to Westinghouse. But Bakelite sales manager Hylton Swan, over an unforgettable lunch, told O'Conor that Bakelite would no longer sell Formica its resin and that Westinghouse was going into the laminate business. O'Conor's immediate reaction went unrecorded by history, but it is known that he quickly looked up Dr. L. V. Redman, a chemist who had been hired by the Chicago-based Karpen Brothers, Adolph and Sam, to improve the varnishes on their furniture. Redmanol, the new resin Redman developed, was immediately made available to Formica, and O'Conor went back to Cincinnati to expand the plant.

The new building was at Spring Grove Avenue and Alabama Street; Bommer and Boschert supplied a new press worth 6,000 on a minimal down payment with a "Pay for it when you can" proviso. Hall Safe and Lock, at the order of company president Hopple, sent Formica a one-ton safe with the words "The Formica Insulation Company" in gold letters on the front. Although the safe was unordered, and although they really had nothing to put in it, it provided a tremendous psychological uplift. Speaking of the morale boost he provided, Hopple said, "You have to take it. Some day you'll be able to pay for it, and that'll be soon enough for us!"[2]

"Formica Freddie" was the son of a Formica Corporation employee. Dressed in bow tie and suspenders, he appeared in several promotional pieces for the company in the early 1950s. *Photo courtesy of Mr. Albert J. Heeb.*

THE LOGO

The Formica trademark follows a course of change and refinement that is familiar to any observer of the history of American logotypes. It is a progression from an oddly harmonious marriage of grace and clunkiness, to a stylish midcentury Modernism, to a rigorously straightforward contemporary look. These changes in the trademark reflect shifts in the way that graphic designers have used and regarded their most basic resource: type.

The earliest company insignia, dating from around 1930—the period when Formica laminate became a consumer product in addition to an industrial one— illustrates a passion for letterforms. The top stroke of the F is an arc, sheltering the rest of the letters, holding them together, acting .

23

Still, with thirty or so people on the payroll by 1915, money was always tight. At one point, they owed Redman $10,000, and Sam Karpen sent Redman to Cincinnati to come back with a check. Again, as legend has it, not only did O'Conor not pay Redman, he got him to extend Formica another $10,000 of credit.

Along with the company's operating premise of "making anything the customer wanted," O'Conor's philosophy—work hard, fight when necessary, and have good friends in business—was implemented. These basic tenets of the company were pushed to the limit throughout the rest of that year. As a result, Kellogg Switchboard, Cutler-Hammer, and Allis-Chalmers Manufacturing all came on board as new

clients. By 1917 sales totaled $75,000, and Formica's business included three components: electrical (insulation), electronic (radio parts, originally manufactured for the Navy), and mechanical (aircraft pulleys, for example). By 1919 Formica was well positioned to take advantage of military as well as civilian contracts, with sales amounting to $175,000. The company required larger facilities, which were purchased (not rented!) at Spring Grove Avenue and Winton Road.

But all was not a bed of roses—there were tough times as well. On June 11, Westinghouse sued Formica on the basis of a patent issued for laminated phenolic canvas. The suit for patent infringement *like the typographic version of a protective, laminated surface. The six letters that follow make up a little hill of type, their tops echoing the contours of the F's fluid top stroke.*

If you look through a book documenting old trademarks, or thumb through the pages of a prewar issue of Fortune, you'll notice dozens of marks that get their distinctive qualities from the often exaggerated shapes of the letters. The commercial artists who created those trademarks were obsessive about their craft and manipulated letterforms lovingly and skillfully. Nobody in the business of creating trademarks worried about maximizing legibility or justifying their aesthetic choices with scientific research. They were simply making a statement and, to the best of their abilities, making it beautiful.

1920s

1930s

1940s

began and ended in District Court, Cincinnati, with the decision that the Westinghouse patent was "invalid because of prior art." Formica had won, but celebration was short-lived. Westinghouse brought two new lawsuits against Formica, one based on rods, tubes, and molded parts, the other based on the 1913 patent assigned to Westinghouse through O'Conor.

The O'Conor case went to the Supreme Court and made legal history when Westinghouse tried to prevent O'Conor from defending himself because it was his patent. Chief Justice William Howard Taft denied the estoppel; Formica won and benefited from considerable good press as journalists around the country

wrote of the David-and-Goliath aspect of the case. With this over, Formica was then sued by Continental Fibre on process patents; the decision came down to whether a particular reinforcement was saturated or coated; again, Formica prevailed.

1940s

1940s

1950s

laminated plastic

1960s

1970s – 1990s

laminate

In its thirty years of service, the original Formica logo appeared in a number of guises. On one early version, the message *Made from Anhydrous Bakelite Resins* runs beneath the word *Formica.* Clearly this was something that the inventors who founded the company thought their customers needed to know. Later the messages became catchier, penned by advertising copywriters and intended to sell. Phrases like *Beauty Bonded, Pays in Performance,* and *At Home with People, At Work in Industry* routinely appeared within the trapezoid that was used to frame the logotype.

During the 1950s the patterns that Raymond Loewy Associates reintroduced for Formica—Skylark, for instance—were exemplars of Modernism. And the logo Loewy's firm created for Formica also exhibits a late–Eisenhower era approach to the Modern. It did not debut, however, until the early Kennedy years (1961). Although its strongest visual element might be mistaken for a wild 1950s coffee table, this updated trademark is also about letterforms; it too is an amplified F. Instead of the first letter embracing the others, the entire logo is an F. The outer strokes are implied by the irregular shape, all acute angles and soft curves, which is commonly referred to as the "anvil." The crossbar of the big F is made from the word *Formica* in a serifed typeface. At the base of this F are the words laminated plastic products, a reminder that Formica must be used as an adjective.

When reproduced in color, the anvil was always red, and when shown in black and white—as in newspaper ads and the

1988

1990

Baekeland had begun suing, too. He sued General Insulate, which molded with Redmanol; he sued Wappler Electric, which used Formica laminate. Something surprising happened, however. Adolph and Sam Karpen bought a two-thirds interest in Condensite Company, giving them numerous laminate patents. Subsequently, Bakelite Company, Condensite Company, and Redmanol Company combined to form the Bakelite Corporation (which later became a part of Union Carbide). From then on, Formica had easy access to Bakelite's materials and technical assistance.

By 1921 Faber and O'Conor's "Vision" was materializing. Formica laminate had been integrated into the home manufacture of radios. Business continued to improve,

and in 1923 Formica got onto solid financial ground for the first time, as timing gears became the newest laminate application. The financial footing stayed firm, but the timing-gear dream turned into a mechanical nightmare soon thereafter. Steven's Motor called O'Conor, saying they had 175 frozen cars in the yard because the Formica timing gears were swelling uncontrollably.

O'Conor moved fast. He hired R. W. Lytle of Moline Plow, an expert in automotive gears. By June of 1924, Lytle and Formica had developed a new combination of varnishes and cotton weaves, with the result that while the gears might still swell from moisture, they at least did so evenly. The Formica team also exerted a strong influence on automobile *phone book—the anvil wore pinstripes. But in 1980, a New York designer named Michael Abramson modified the Loewy logo in order, as it says in the corporate graphics standards manual, to "assist in reproduction."*

In corporate identity design, there is an unwritten rule that any extraneous detail will make a logo too complicated to read at a glance. In the case of the Formica logo, this view caused the elimination of the striped version and the substitution of Helvetica for the serifed face Loewy used. Helvetica was in 1980, and still is, the favorite typeface of corporations and institutions. Its clear, regular forms represent an unromantic, functionalist philosophy of type that is the antithesis of the attitude demonstrated by the original logo. In 1930 the letters of the word

Formica were supposed to exude style. Fifty years later, they were there simply to be read—not admired. In the 1980 design, it is the anvil that is visually important and memorable.

Karrie Jacobs

motor design, predicting a change involving the use of air vents to carry off water vapors. The change was adopted, and many of the auto manufacturers of the time, impressed by Formica's engineering acumen, used Formica's gears. Sales jumped to $1,900,000 in 1923; the next year they topped $3,000,000. The company churned out up to 6,000 timing gears per day for a historical roster of clients, including Auburn, Buick, McFarlane, Nash, Pontiac, Studebaker, and Willys-Overland.

During these years, technological lessons learned in the automotive field were quickly applied to the emerging consumer appliance industry. Washing machines, vacuum cleaners, and refrigerators all came

under scrutiny, and all benefited in performance and economics by shifting to Formica parts. Formica also developed the Gyro-Tex bobbin, a standard for many years in the synthetic textile field, and began experimenting with a decorative laminate printing process.

Faber realized that although black was selling well, changes were afoot in the decorative application of laminate. He pushed marble patterns into production, and they were used in the beginning of 1925 as replacements for metal strips on soda fountains for customers like Liquid Carbonic Corporation, then a giant in the field. To begin to meet the need for new laminate applications, Faber found an up-and-coming scientist at MIT named Jack

1-7

Timing gears made by the Formica Company were used in automobiles such as this 1927 Buick model. *Photo courtesy of Buick.*

1-8

This 1925 advertisement asked customers to "Come to Headquarters" with problems they thought "might be solved by the application of a laminated phenolic material." In its early days, the company's basic premise was: "Whatever the customer wants, try to make it, no matter what it is."

1-9

A mid-1920s advertisement for the Formica Insulation Company, when timing gears became an application for laminated plastics. At one point, the company manufactured 6,000 timing gears a day.

Cochrane, who later became Director of Research. The company was running well, profits were continually plowed back into operations, and Faber and O'Conor were sitting atop an expanding physical plant.

This condition led to a corporate reorganization; the 600 shares were converted to no-par-value stock at a 300-1 ratio. Then 18,000 of the new 180,000 shares were offered to the public. The price opened at $16.50 and within weeks was up to $25 per share.

In 1926 Formica added another key player—George H. Clark, another MIT graduate, who was brought on board to create a state-of-the-art factory. This became increasingly critical because Bakelite's basic patents expired in 1926 and 1927, and other companies rushed into the laminate business, including Monsanto, National Vulcanized Fibre (both in 1922), Synthane Corporation (1928), and the Spaulding Fibre Company (1923). Even as Formica raced toward record-breaking sales, competitive products, such as Westinghouse's Micarta, threatened the company's corporate longevity.

In 1927 Formica turned the tables on its competitors. The company's future changed for the richer with U.S. patents 1,863,239 and 1,904,718, which allowed "lithographed woodgrains of light color, employing an opaque barrier sheet to block out the dark interior of the laminate sheet" to be produced on a flat-bed press. It was Formica's version of "The Big Idea," and technical improvements quickly followed, for example, continuous designs were developed on gravure cylinders, rendering the flat-bed press obsolete. This was the beginning of the modern Formica era, and the big news was decorative sheets.

In 1931 three more patents were received by Formica for the preparation of the first all-paper-based laminate, and for the addition of a layer of aluminum foil between the core and the surface, making the laminate cigarette-proof. During this time, Formica salesmen played a key role in spreading the word about what the new decorative material could do. This was very important, since at that time there was no existing precedent for the material and its potential.

In the middle of the depression of the 1930s, Formica's business slipped drastically to less than half of what it had been two years earlier. Nonetheless, Faber and O'Conor, like true entrepreneurs still, increased spending on advertising, engineering, and research. They also implemented a three-point policy of management: Everything will be made on order only; everything will be inspected; and everything will be delivered on time. For Formica in the 1930s, customer satisfaction and product quality were job one.

In 1935 the company, pushed externally by concern for its well-being and internally by its stretched personnel resources, reorganized for the first time, with Faber as Chairman of the Board, O'Conor as President and Secretary, Walter Kraus as Assistant Secretary, and Walter Gebhart as Treasurer. A major flood hit Cincinnati and Formica in 1937, damaging the first-floor ceiling, and after the cleanup, Faber was felled by a severe heart attack. As a result, his schedule was much reduced. The company was re-forming in the process; the gear- and insulation-based caterpillar was turning into a decoratively patterned butterfly.

O'Conor pushed his employees to innovate. Realwood was introduced, a laminate with genuine wood veneer mounted on a paper lamination with a heat-reactive binder. Even more significantly, Formica replaced thio-resin with melamine resin (from American Cyanamid, which in the mid-1950s would acquire Formica), allowing for better looks and greater machinability and durability. With these improvements, kitchen table and dinette manufacturers started using Formica laminate for tabletops—the introduction of decorative laminates into the furniture and consumer markets.

Even though World War II saw only industrial grades of Formica laminate produced, sales in 1940 were $4,251,109, sales in the following year were almost double that, and by 1943, sales almost doubled again to $15,736,768. Formica products found many wartime uses. Pregwood, a laminated plastic material composed of wood veneers and resin, was used as an aluminum replacement in some aircraft. There were, for instance, some eighty-eight separate Formica laminate pieces in the P-51 fighter plane alone!

After the war, Formica turned to a booming residential construction and dinette industry and developed the first postformable melamine-surfaced laminate. O'Conor, who had been with Formica during the transition from a war economy to a peace economy, set the tone for expansion into new and existing·markets. He picked homes, schools, and public buildings as obvious targets. Soon after, Formica also set the standard in the printed circuit and miniaturization businesses.

In 1947 a license agreement was drawn up with the De La Rue Company of

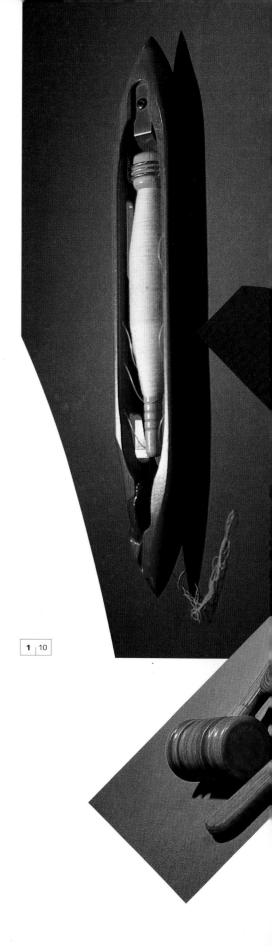

1-10
Formica laminate objects
from the 1930s included
loom shuttles, knife
handles, gavels, and
brushes for
non-industrial use.

London, and Formica licensed European manufacturing and marketing rights to the British firm until 1977. Also during this time, Formica developed a dull-rubbing technique that better simulated woods for manufacturers of high-quality furniture. In recognition of the direction the company was moving (away from electrical insulation) and in light of the way the "Vision" was being reformulated, Formica Insulation Company officially changed its name to The Formica Company.

As the 1950s began, distributors started to warehouse stocks of Formica laminate, ending up with sizable furniture accounts, and this opened the door for competitors to begin to sell directly to the public. In 1951 Formica responded to the surging market by constructing and opening (at George Clark's urging) a state-of-the-art 1,000,000-square-foot plant in Evendale (a suburb of Cincinnati) devoted exclusively to the production of decorative sheet material. A new removable wall installation system was employed, allowing for future expansion, and significant capital improvement took place in the form of new tools and machinery. If, for America, the 1940s were about a yearning for comfort, the 1950s were about satisfying that need, a need that Formica incorporated into its expanded vision. The 1950s, according to *A Concise Guide to Plastics,* were a time when "[plastic grew] more rapidly than most other American industries and [expanded] at an astonishing rate."[3]

The Formica Company was no exception. In 1950 a two-for-one stock split took place. Sales reached more than $24,000,000 in 1951, and in 1952, postforming started to be widely used in new schools for classroom counter tops. In 1956, after its purchase by American Cyanamid, the company became Formica Corporation, a subsidiary of American Cyanamid (which not coincidentally had a long history of plastic production, including Russel Wright's melamine dinnerware of the mid-forties).

While Formica laminate was not born in the 1950s, it did come of age then, as did lava lamps, kidney-shaped tables, sweater girls, coffee shops, diners, TV dinners, and a series of recently introduced miracle materials such as Dacron, melamine, nylon, Orlon, polyethylene, and polystyrene. It was a time when the fabric of life, literally, was changing, when Ray Kroc's restaurant called McDonald's was born, when the interstate highway system was truly conceptualized, when Disneyland opened, when the Boeing 707 was introduced, and when the drive-in theater reached its apotheosis.[4]

1-11
An early laminate press.

1-12
By the 1950s, large-scale machinery was employed to produce Formica brand plastic laminate. The laminate sheets shown here were, however, the same impregnated kraft paper.

1-13
A view of Formica's factory during the 1930s. The company's production of many industrial goods required a large labor force.

The magnitude of these changes was enormous. Chester Liebs reports of drive-in movie theaters, "Whereas a handful of screens had existed in 1946, more than 1,700 screen towers loomed over the roadside landscape by 1950."[5] The exteriors of these drive-ins were all vivacious curves, funky type, and "boom-boom" colors, but on the inside, Liebs notes, "the interiors began to exhibit innovative materials such as glistening mother-of-pearl Formica and sheets of etched translucent plastic."[6] It was not only mother-of-pearl patterns that exemplified this time, but also the ultra-fifties speckled patterns (usually with a whitish background) and the Skylark pattern (reintroduced in 1989 and now called Boomerang), which typified the polymorphic design language of the period.

Formica laminate found many unusual end uses at this time. The first ski prototypes using Formica laminate , for example, were produced by Howard Head, of Head Sporting Goods, in the 1950s. Head's first skis were made of aluminum (which replaced wood) from Martin Aircraft Company and had bottoms covered with shiny black Formica laminate. The aluminum/laminate skis were doomed, however, once high-molecular-weight polyethylene replaced the Formica laminate.

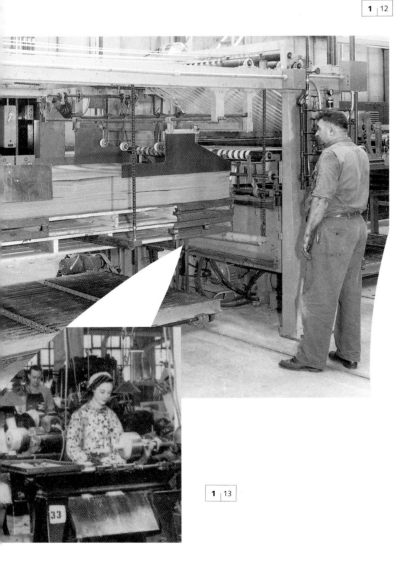

1 | 12

1 | 13

Artist Jack Lilly devised another unusual end use for Formica laminate: He used it as a base on which to paint airbrushed murals at such places as the Acton Lake Park Lodge in Houston State Park, in effect creating yet another kind of "laminate art." In the mid-1950s, Formica also started making custom colors and patterns in-house—for example, the custom design created for the Chicago, Milwaukee, and St. Paul Railroad (see Simon Leung's sidebar on Brooks Stevens in chapter 4). Everything pointed straight ahead into the future toward faster material development, acceleration of style and taste, and a countrywide spread of laminated lifestyles.

In 1960 the fully mature Formica Corporation embraced an intensive product development program, building a 40,000-square-foot Research and Design Center in Evendale, the efforts of which culminated in 1964 with the introduction of the Formica World's Fair House in Flushing Meadow, Queens, New York. (The kitchen from the World's Fair House was rebuilt for the Queens Museum's 1989 exhibition "Remembering the Future: The New York World's Fairs from 1939 to 1964.") Made entirely of Formica laminate, the World's Fair House propagated a living environment fabricated in a single material, a single idea. Seen from this point of view, it was the first signal of Formica's commitment to architectural design concepts in years to come.

In the spirit of the early 1960s, the World's Fair House focused on displaying and celebrating contemporary American achievements. Formica's contribution was an optimistic riot of decorator colors, a Native American–inspired laminate

31

bedroom, and a bevy of crayon-proof, easy-cleaning, easy-living surfaces designed for "durable beauty." Needless to say, the house was very popular with the visitors to the fairgrounds.

To take advantage of booming growth in the western United States, Formica Corporation built its Sierra Plant in 1966 outside Sacramento, California, thereby becoming a truly national company with ever-growing international ambition. With its production capacity rising by 30 percent, Formica Corporation was armed for the first time since the end of World War II with a production capacity equal to demand. As a member of The Color Council, Formica made strong attempts to coordinate its new and existing laminate colors with those of the large and small appliance industries.

In 1969 a Design Center (now known as the Gordon Sterling Building, named for the president/chairman of the company from 1981 to 1988) responsible for coming up with new designs, colors, and special effects was created during an overall building expansion that added the complete capability to make laminate samples for testing and evaluation to the Research & Development Center. A year later, the inevitable finally happened. What had been Formica's starting point came to an end as the production of industrial-grade laminate ceased; simultaneously, Formica withdrew from the molding business and began pushing its laminate beyond traditional markets.

In 1971 a new patent was awarded for the development of a heavy-ink process used as another surface texturing technique, while one year later, a metallic laminate line was produced as a special-effects range for commercial applications.

For years, Formica was the only company to do its own printing—a high-fidelity rotogravure process whereby patterns were created in-house and then stored until the laminate was made.

Formica entered the low-pressure-laminate market in 1973, opening a production plant in Tarboro, North Carolina. More significantly, the word *design* started to show up in external and internal corporate communications of the time; "Leadership by Design" had long been the company's slogan, but in 1973 it started to pack some punch. In the late seventies this was formalized with the establishment of the Design Advisory Board (DAB).[7]

1-14
The company's promotional poster for its World's Fair House of 1964. Built on a man-made hill at the 1964 New York World's Fair site, the house was an example of a livable environment for the nuclear family in Suburbia, U.S.A.

1-15
The "Vanitory" was a marketing idea based on turning the bathroom sink into a piece of furniture.
Photo: Tom Treick.

1 | 14

Using design as part of an increasingly complex marketing strategy, the DAB was a design think tank. It asked Formica's management to reexamine its commitment to aesthetics, and urged them to consider launching a solid-color-throughout laminate. Since the 1950s, researchers in Formica's labs had experimented with an all-solid laminate. As part of an effort to tap a design-based market for these integral surfaces, Formica came up with its solid laminate, called ColorCore, in 1982. With ColorCore, Formica Corporation entered the 1980s' design world. Formica chairman Vincent P. Langone, who was director of marketing at the time, orchestrated a product launch of such historic proportions

1 | 15

that just two years later the ColorCore name was recognized by eighty percent of architects and designers, according to a Yankelovich, Skelly & White market survey.

Along with its Italian competitor, Abet Laminati, Formica brought laminates to prominence globally. This participation in the international design community reflected Formica laminate's international appeal. Almost every one of the sundry experiments and design exhibitions Formica sponsored in the eighties, including "Surface & Ornament" and "Material Evidence: New Color Techniques in Handmade Furniture," traveled outside the United States and engaged the talents of designers and architects abroad. Laminates constituted both a trend in decoration and a movement in design; Formica laminate was no longer just a paradigmatic industrial material but also a blank canvas upon which creative events were staged. Designers from all over the world used ColorCore, and later Surell® solid surfacing material, in everything from architecture and furniture to art jewelry.

In terms of the company's corporate direction, Formica Corporation's senior managers, along with private investors, bought the company from its parent, American Cyanamid, in a leveraged buyout in 1985. By mid-1987 Formica once again became a publicly traded company with a listing on the New York Stock Exchange.

The company remained public until May 1989, when management decided to take the company private. With more than 50 percent of its sales derived from international operations, Formica continues to be the largest laminate producer in the world, with factories in the United States, England, France, Spain, Canada, and Taiwan.

On the museum front, Formica gained new respectability in the 1980s. For the Washington, D.C. National Museum of American History's 1987 exhibition "A Material World," curator Robert Post, diner historian Richard J. S. Gutman, and exhibit designer Jeff Howard discovered and resurrected a vintage, 1940s-era diner and used it as the centerpiece of the exhibition. It displayed all the elements that conjure our nostalgia for the roadside diner: colored enamel bands of stainless steel on the exterior, vinyl seats and stools, ceramic tiles, and, of course, counters made with Formica laminate.[8] By the 1980s, mass-produced objects such as counters crafted with Formica laminate had gained enough currency to qualify as collectible materials of

1 | 16

35

historical value. Part of this was certainly due to the product's adaptability. From its status as an avant-garde material in the 1930s to its reincarnation as the ultimate symbol of Americana in the 1950s, Formica laminate's image changed with each era to suit the circumstances.

In the present postmodern era, characterized by a commitment to surface and to the superficial in all the senses, Formica laminate is a material without par. By both covering and revealing, and by showing a remarkable commitment to depth in its thin surface, Formica laminate has not simply weathered the trend toward layering and eclecticism, it has been integral to it. Its ability to be whatever we want it to be has made Formica laminate an uncommon material. In the postmodern era, form has stopped following function. Now, form follows whatever it wants, including laminates.

Form following Formica laminate should not surprise us. In the end, the history of Formica laminate is not what any of us would think. Far from being a fifties flash in the pan, it has been a vitally important material phenomenon. Throughout this Plastic Century, our acceptance, purchase, and use of plastics have continually outpaced our knowledge of what these new materials were. Laminate, though, has always seemed understandable, even user-friendly. What do you think lies so serenely beneath the spill in Rosie's diner in the Bounty paper-towel commercials? From its early days as a purely functional material used to replace timing gears, commutator rings, and bobbins to its most recent postmodern heyday, Formica laminate has traveled a path unlike any other material in this century.

It has been whatever we have wanted or needed it to be. Up, down, and all around, it has been used on big boats (H.M.S. *Queen Mary*), in big spaces (the Library of Congress), big places (the United Airlines Terminal at O'Hare International Airport), and big-deal furniture (in Radio City Music Hall), and has made big splashes—as in the Regent Palace Hotel's cocktail lounge in London, where "everything possible was made of gleaming Formica, from tabletops and wall surfaces to the armrests of the couches. . . ."[9]

1-18
Elgin Diner, Camden, New Jersey.
Photo: R. J. S. Gutman.

1-19
Boundbrook Diner, Boundbrook, New Jersey.
Decorative inlay (detail) using Formica laminate.
Photo: R. J. S. Gutman.

1 | 18

Notes

1 *Formica: Forty Years of Steady Vision* (The Formica Company, 1953), limited edition. Much of the information in this chapter, particularly regarding the history of Formica's early years, is drawn liberally from this "official history." Where specific information is taken, citation is made.

2 Ibid.

3 *A Concise Guide to Plastics* (New York: Reinhold Publishing Corp., 1960).

4 Kenneth I. Helphand, "McUrbia: The 1950s and the Birth of the Contemporary American Landscape," *Places* 5, 40.

5 Chester Liebs, *From Main Street to Miracle Mile* (Boston: Little, Brown, 1985), 160.

6 Ibid.

7 Edward Lebow, "Formica Seeks to Expand Market by Wooing Designers," *Industrial Design* (January/February 1983), 12.

8 Dena Kleiman, "Smithsonian Gives New Life to Old Diner," *New York Times*, 17 June 1987, B1.

9 Sylvia Katz, *Plastics: Designs and Materials* (London: Cassell & Collier Macmillan, Ltd., 1978), 62.

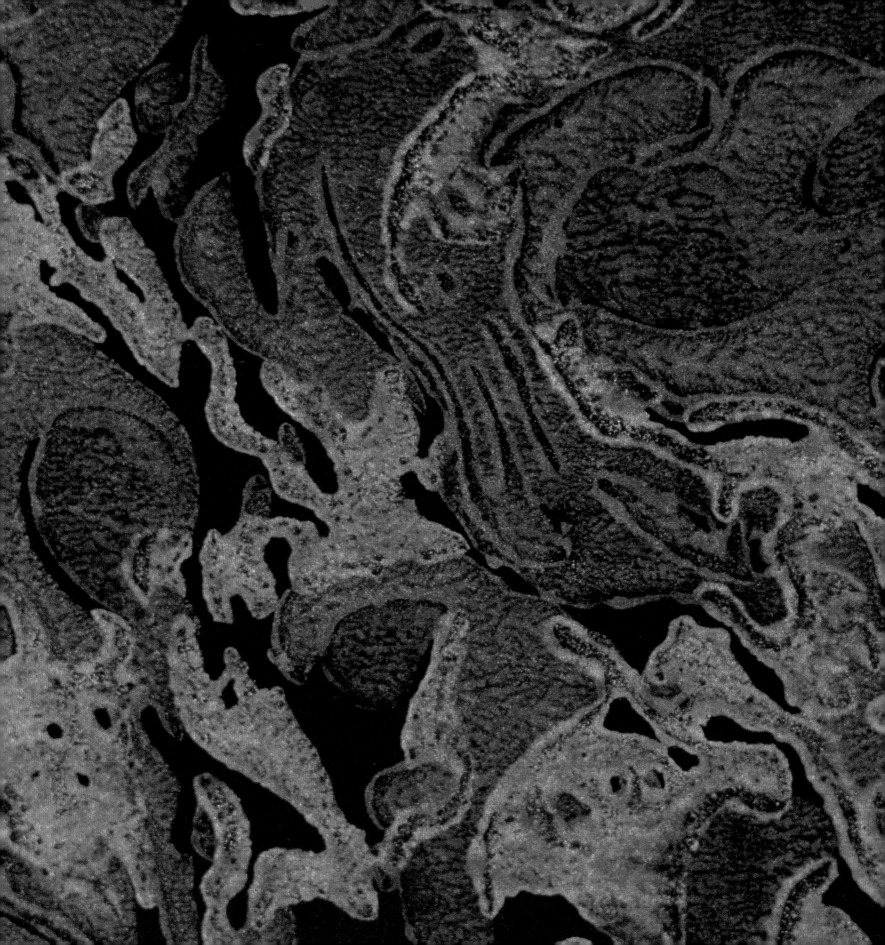

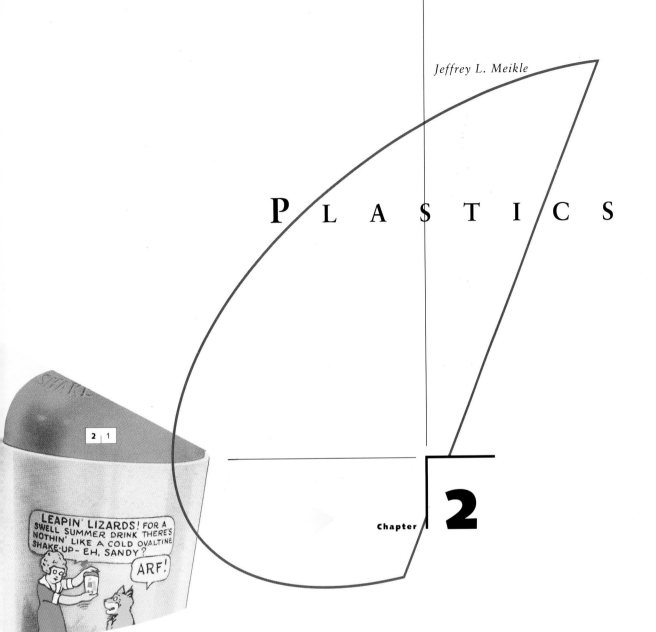

Jeffrey L. Meikle

P L A S T I C S

Chapter **2**

Nothing is more natural this late in the twentieth century than the synthetic materials that surround us—materials whose colors, surfaces, textures, and tactile qualities would have seemed wholly *un*natural when the century was young. As Roland Barthes once observed in a meditation on the ubiquity of plastic, it sometimes appears as if "the whole world *can* be plasticized" or brought under control through an infinitely malleable medium. This observation, dating from the

mid-1950s, when applications of new materials indeed proliferated at an unprecedented rate, suggests a feeling of vertigo. The response to plastic was not always so apprehensive, however. Two decades earlier, during the 1930s, journalists and publicists had proclaimed the utopian significance of plastic. Transmuted by wonder-working chemists from such

2-1
This Plaskon "Orphan Annie Cold Ovaltine Shake-up Mug" was originally introduced in 1933. *Photo: Kurz-Kasch, Inc./ Martin Biel.*

2 | 2

2-2
Visions of Utopia. Buildings from the 1939 New York World's Fair embodied the influence of streamlining and a faith in technological progress. *Photos courtesy of City of New York, Parks and Recreation Photo Archives.*

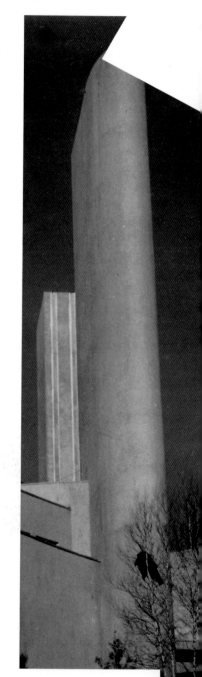

environments, that most directly embodied the machine-age aesthetic of the era and its search for controlled certainty. Such places as automats, chain stores, theaters, and nightclubs offered artificial precision in flawless surfaces of smooth Formica laminate, deep mirrors of jade green or jet black deceptively reflecting a futuristic "polished orderly essential" that remained a dream in the real world of the 1930s. Recent nostalgic interest in the plastic objects and environments of that decade, including those fabricated of Formica laminate, indicates the lingering attractiveness of that vision now that our culture has become too complex to entertain it seriously.[1]

Although plastics were just emerging during the 1930s as glamorous design materials for consumer products and environments, they had long served in hidden electrical and mechanical applications essential to machine-age expansion, primarily as insulation in dynamos, motors, distributor caps, radio panels and tubes, and as noiseless gears in automotive starters and timers. The origin of laminate itself lay not in a desire for decorative surfacing materials but in the early electrical industry's urgent need for insulating materials impervious to oils, acids, humidity, and temperature extremes. Laminate's beginning is inseparable from that of Bakelite, the first truly synthetic plastic, invented in 1907 by Leo Baekeland. At that time the only existing plastic as we now define the word was celluloid, a compound of nitrocellulose and camphor used since 1869 as a substitute for ivory, tortoiseshell, and horn. Its sensitivity to mild heat made it perfect for molding combs, small toys, and other inexpensive consumer

common natural substances as coal, air, and water, plastic promised to usher in a democratic era of limitless material abundance. Many people, as tired of economic panaceas as of the Great Depression itself, may have skimmed over magazine articles about new miracle materials, but they could not ignore the evidence of their senses. Substantial innovation marked many material aspects of everyday life. Lustrous streamlined Plaskon radios, glossily colored Catalin jewelry, telephones and office machines of polished Bakelite: These and other manifestations of plastic offered a promise of ongoing transformation. But perhaps it was Formica laminate, when used as a finishing material in commercial

2 | 4

2 | 4

2-3
This ivory Bakelite
telephone was used on
the luxury ocean liner
H. M. S. Queen Mary,
in the 1930s.
*Photo courtesy of
Ken Schultz,
Hoboken, NJ.*

2-4
Bakelite found its early
applications in objects
such as this clock
and hair comb.
*Photos: © David Arky
1989.*

goods but useless for industrial applications requiring dimensional stability; celluloid also suffered from flammability. The other major "plastics" in use early in this century included the natural materials hard rubber (from the milky latex of the rubber tree) and shellac (from the secretions of an East Indian insect). The fast-growing electrical industry relied on hard rubber for molded insulators. It also relied on shellac as a varnish for insulating wire coils and, crucial to the development of Formica laminate, for impregnating layers of paper that were compressed into strong, lightweight armatures and winding tubes. Bakelite—a hard condensation product of phenol and formaldehyde that was resistant to heat, water, chemicals, and electric current— largely replaced both hard rubber and shellac for electrical insulation. In fact, Baekeland's discovery resulted from a direct attempt to synthesize an impregnating resin that was better than shellac.[2]

43

Even before receiving patent protection for his discovery of June 1907, Baekeland sought to exploit it by testing potential commercial applications in his own small laboratory (he was an independent consulting chemist) and by sharing the results with engineers from selected companies. During 1907–08 he experimented with such Formica laminate forerunners as "polished Bakalite fiberboard," "Bakalized pulpboard," "Bakalite floor tiles," and phonograph records made "by impregnating paper with Bakelite and then compressing [it] under mould at high temperature." By the time he publicly announced his discovery in February 1909, Baekeland had already promoted his material for such diverse purposes as billiard balls and cutlery handles but had attracted only one serious customer, the Boonton Rubber Company, which sought an improvement on the hard rubber from which it molded electrical insulators. That situation soon changed. An engineer at Westinghouse, Dr. C. E. Skinner, had seen an article published by Baekeland in January 1910 that described impregnation and hardening of paper. Looking for a substitute for shellac in the company's laminated Micarta insulation board, Skinner wrote to Baekeland and in April received a free sample of eighteen pounds of liquid Bakelite with which to experiment. Within two weeks Westinghouse had ordered three hundred pounds more at cost. Two months later, when Skinner and a Westinghouse associate named Sanborn visited Baekeland "to learn more about Bakelite," the inventor himself was thinking of manufacturing "Bakelite paper." This never came to pass, however, for in the following year Westinghouse became a major consumer of Bakelite, along with Boonton Rubber and General Electric. While Baekeland continued to pour time and money into such diversions as phonograph records, imitation-amber pipe stems, and an ill-fated molding compound that used ground vegetable ivory as a filler, the "laminating varnish business expanded rapidly" because, as an associate recalled, Westinghouse "knew a good thing when they saw it." That "good thing" became Formica laminate.[3]

The Formica Insulation Company began in Cincinnati in 1913 as a shoestring venture of two former Westinghouse employees, Daniel J. O'Conor and Herbert A. Faber. While working under Skinner as a research engineer at Westinghouse, O'Conor had perfected a process for making rigid laminated sheets from kraft paper and liquid Bakelite. Continuous ribbons of paper passed through a bath of liquid Bakelite and then into and through a drying chamber before being cut into dry, resin-impregnated sheets. Stacked in layers and compressed between the heated plates of a flat-bed hydraulic press, where final curing of the synthetic resin occurred, the former paper sheets emerged as a single rigid laminated sheet with the chemical and electrical properties of Bakelite, ready to be cut into the required shapes. Aware of the market for electrical insulation, O'Conor and his partner, who had worked in the sales department at Westinghouse, hoped to capitalize on their knowledge of the product that Westinghouse was then referring to as "Bakelite-Micarta" to distinguish it from the inferior shellac-impregnated "Micarta." It was a short distance, but an imaginative one, from "Micarta" to "Formica."

Under pressure from his major customer—Westinghouse—to squelch the renegade Formica, Baekeland refused to sell liquid resin to O'Conor and Faber, except for use in laminated tubes and rods, thus forcing them to buy from the equally upstart Redmanol Company, an infringer of Baekeland's basic resin patent. In 1922 Bakelite finally absorbed its competitors Redmanol and Condensite, but Formica enjoyed no similar resolution of its situation. Westinghouse, General Electric, and the smaller independents Continental Fibre and Diamond State Fibre all competed with Formica in manufacturing and selling essentially the same product. In the meantime, Westinghouse had introduced its Bakelite-Micarta-D, made of impregnated layers of cotton duck instead of kraft paper, which yielded blanks for the cutting of noiseless gears. Formica correctly concluded that the patent for Bakelite-Micarta-D was indefensible and began to manufacture its own gear stock; however,

paper laminates remained the company's major product. With the advent of radio, Formica laminate finally began not only to distinguish itself from its competitors but also, like other plastics, to rise from its submerged status as an industrial material into the highly visible realm of consumer goods.[4]

Although the young plastics industry grew along with automotive expansion, it was radio that eventually brought such plastics as Formica laminate and Bakelite into the American parlor. By 1915 considerable amounts of Formica laminate went into large radio sets for commercial shipping and naval vessels. Most sets were assembled on Formica laminate mounting tables that effectively insulated coils, tuners, and other parts from one another. But the typical radio set also possessed a highly visible front panel on which its molded Bakelite dials were mounted—an expanse of black Formica laminate whose flawless gleaming surface derived from highly polished stainless-steel plates used in the material's final compression. Military demand for radio sets during World War I strained manufacturing capacity, but the true radio boom came between 1920 and 1924, when Formica's annual sales increased from $400,000 to $3 million. The company owed much of this increase to civilian radio enthusiasts who assembled their own sets at home. A salesman, Edwin M. Wolcott, later recalled "the great radio 'do-it-yourself' boom" by exclaiming, "What a difference, no peddling, just taking orders." As radio sets became domesticated, they had to harmonize with traditional furniture, and Formica responded to the demand by offering brown panels in addition to the standard black. In 1924 chemist Clarence M. Hargrave began to develop a process for incorporating a "wood-grain" lithograph as the top layer in a laminate sheet. Not marketed until 1927, wood-grain Formica laminate arrived too late for radio hobbyists and was as yet too crude in appearance for use on furniture or interiors. By then the company was on the verge of losing much of its radio market for a reason that reveals a crucial distinction between laminates and other plastics. As plastic molding techniques became more sophisticated during the 1930s, radio cabinets molded complete in one piece became the norm. Plastic moldings enabled manufacturers to consolidate parts, to reduce assembly costs, and to offer curvilinear products whose streamlined forms expressed the machine age. Formica laminate, by contrast, required fabrication by skilled workers. No matter how expressive its smooth, precise, gleaming surface, Formica laminate remained in application a labor-intensive pre-machine-age material. In fact, it remains even today a relatively low-tech material used not only by contractors and carpenters but also by do-it-yourselfers—something that can be said of few other plastics.[5]

Although a fundamental gulf thus separated Formica laminate from other plastics, the products made from these materials shared many problems during the 1930s, most notably that of color. As early as 1927 the Hotel Manger of New York had furnished each room with a chiffonier whose fold-down writing surface was inlaid with stain-proof black laminate—necessary, according to one account, because Prohibition had driven guests out of the lounge and into their rooms to drink. Such applications foreshadowed Formica laminate's emergence as a major decorative surfacing material. But the color black had passed into stylistic oblivion with the Model T, and consumers were demanding an assortment of light colors in products of all kinds. Only dark surface layers of brown and green paper could successfully conceal the dark, industrial-strength resin at the

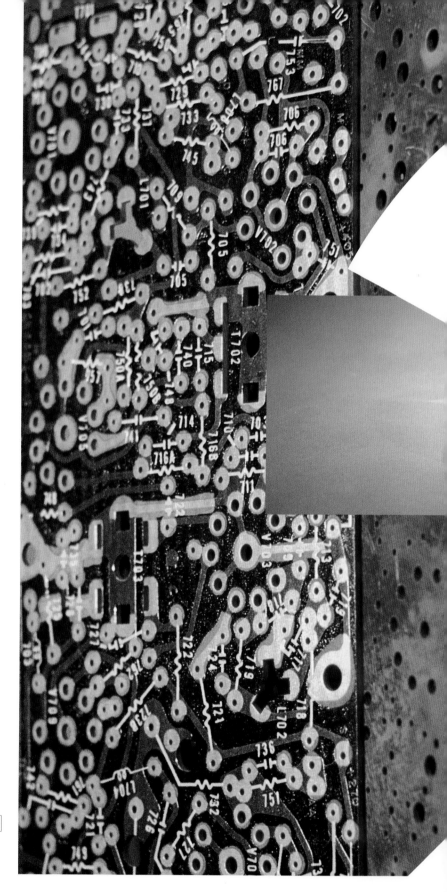

2-5
Formica Corporation
manufactured many
industrial objects before
its entry into the
consumer-goods market.
Shown here are an
electrical board and a
Halliborton ball valve
for oil wells.

the 1930s well publicized in architecture
and design magazines, decorative plastic
laminate emerged as the surfacing material
par excellence for Woolworth service
counters, cafeterias, cocktail lounges,
Checker cabs, streamliner coaches, and
other public spaces of the machine age—as
well as for custom furniture and interiors
designed by Paul Frankl, Gilbert Rohde, and
Donald Deskey for Manhattan's wealthy
avant-garde.[6]

2 | 5

core of every sheet of Formica laminate.
Seeking a solution to the challenge of light
colors, the company kept chemist Jack
Cochrane busy from 1928 to 1939. His
progress followed that of much of the
plastics industry, which had remained
equally dependent on dark phenol
formaldehyde resins. Molders of plastic also
sought a light-colored material with
properties similar to those of Bakelite, a
need filled in 1931 with the Toledo
Synthetic Products Company's
announcement of Plaskon, a urea-
formaldehyde resin that soon turned up in
radio cabinets, bottle stoppers, and Orphan
Annie Ovaltine shakers. At about the same
time, Cochrane succeeded in developing a
decorative laminate whose top layer of
paper was impregnated not with phenol but
with urea, and then laminated under
pressure to the phenol-impregnated papers
underneath. The result, a hard, relatively
durable, fire-resistant, easily cleaned
surfacing material available in virtually any
color desired, won commissions for major
decorative applications. Gray pearlized
Formica laminate graced the liner H.M.S.
Queen Mary, while green morocco Formica
laminate soothed visitors to the new Library
of Congress annex. With those successes of

47

2 | 7

2 | 6

2-6
Formica laminate panels
covered the walls of the
lobby of the A. O. Smith
corporate headquarters,
built by the Chicago
architecture firm
Holabird & Root.
*Photo: Hedrich-Blessing,
Chicago.*

2-7
The observation lounge
of the ocean liner
H. M. S. Queen Mary.
Gray "Pearl" Formica
laminate was used
extensively on the
ship's interior.
*Photo courtesy of
Frank Braynard.*

2-8
Decorative plastic
laminate was the
preferred surfacing
material for railroad
coach interiors.
*Photo courtesy of
Union Pacific.*

49

Although the cultural elite ironically
preferred black, with its evocation of
mechanical precision, the company offered
dozens of colors and finishes, light or dark,
glossy or matte, pearlized or marbleized,
wood-grained or linen-textured. However,
the high cost of processing urea-
formaldehyde Formica laminate prevented
true democratization of the material. Final
curing required such precise temperature
control that thermocouples had to be
embedded within each sheet of laminate.
Cochrane continued to search for an
impregnating resin that would permit
manufacture of light shades of laminate at
reasonable cost. Meanwhile he introduced
such refinements as cigarette-burn-proof
Formica laminate with a layer of foil

embedded under the top layer of paper to disperse heat over a wide area and thus prevent charring. Eventually, in 1938, the company replaced urea-formaldehyde resin with a new plastic, melamine, that had been developed in Britain as a material for unbreakable dishes and that was being marketed in the United States by American Cyanamid. As before, the new laminate consisted of a base of seven layers of kraft paper impregnated with phenol-formaldehyde resin; now, however, the decorative layer was impregnated with melamine and topped with an opaque sheet, also impregnated with melamine, that became transparent when cured in the press. Melamine proved to be a plastic resin more durable than urea formaldehyde, far easier and thus cheaper to cure, and stable in color even when used with the most light-colored decorative papers. As O'Conor observed, it "made decorative [laminate] a permanent material . . . that we could stand [in] back of." [7]

Pioneering the route later taken by the entire plastics industry during the 1950s, when lower resin prices and new thermoplastic materials derived from petroleum enabled true proliferation among the general public of goods made of polyethylene, polystyrene, and vinyl, the company moved quickly to exploit the market potential for inexpensive melamine laminate. In the process Formica laminate took on its most characteristic guise as a surfacing material for kitchen counter tops and dinettes. As early as 1939 the company sold sheets to Chicago furniture makers who produced the first dinettes, intended to replace those of white porcelain-enameled steel whose finishes marred too easily,

2-9
Interior views of Radio City Music Hall.
Donald Deskey designed the furniture which has been installed in the lobby since the 1930s.
Photos: Bo Parker, New York, NY.

2-10
Formica laminate was used to surface radio cabinets in the 1930s, but was soon replaced by molded plastics.

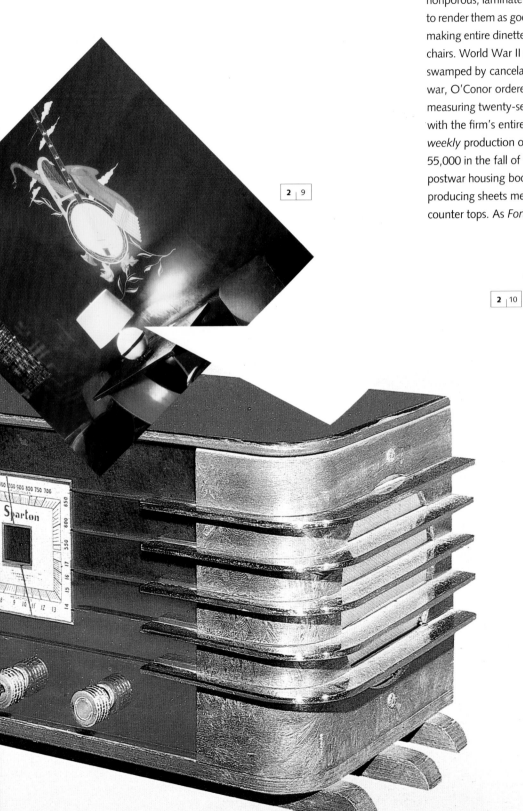

leaving ugly black patches beneath. Not only durable but also nonporous, laminate dinettes required only the wipe of a damp cloth to render them as good as new. Within a short time the company was making entire dinette tops for sale to distributors who added legs and chairs. World War II only postponed the expansion. In April 1945, swamped by cancelations of government orders at the end of the war, O'Conor ordered new press plates for making "dinette sheets" measuring twenty-seven by sixty inches. By the summer of 1948, with the firm's entire resources devoted to decorative laminate, *weekly* production of dinette sheets reached 28,000 units; it rose to 55,000 in the fall of 1950. The company had also anticipated the postwar housing boom by acquiring a giant press capable of producing sheets measuring thirty by ninety-six inches for kitchen counter tops. As *Fortune* reported in 1951, the Formica Company

2 | 9

2 | 10

51

was leading "in the scramble to satisfy the urgent demand for decorative plastic table tops and kitchen sinks." By this point Formica laminate had become a technically mature product; it subsequently changed little. Its surface designs changed frequently, however, encompassing not only plastic's traditional function of imitation but also suggesting the American culture's fascination with endlessly remolding a malleable environment. Formica laminate's amoeboid and boomerang patterns, its metallic flecks, and other innovative jet-age effects, reflected this concern by almost literally mirroring the three-dimensional shapes of the molded products that plastic enabled the postwar generation to enjoy. Both expressions proved equally—and endlessly—ephemeral.[8]

To place laminate in the context of plastic in general leads to paradox. The uniqueness of laminate among the plastics lies in its flatness. Substance merges with surface. Volume dissolves, becomes unreal. This quality distinguishes laminate from plastic but also reveals the very essence of plastic. Consider first the radical distinction. Other plastics, those that are molded, foamed, or extruded, possess tremendous plasticity of form. Freed from the limitations of natural materials, we can make from plastic any three-dimensional shape we can imagine. In a design sense, plastic indeed grants us the material liberation promised by "plastic utopians" of the 1930s.[9] The potential of flat, two-dimensional Formica laminate pales by comparison. On the other hand, consider laminate's fundamental identity with plastic: the penchant for imitative surfaces. Makers of celluloid developed complex processes for imitating

2-11
Formica laminate found applications in the food-service and hotel industries. Owners of "modern" restaurants in the 1930s began replacing wooden tabletops with the wipe-clean product.

2-12
Advertisements for Formica laminate tabletops of the 1940s.

2-13
A Formica laminate mural designed and fabricated in 1986 by Sheila Klein, Ries Niemi and Norman Millar (A2Z, Los Angeles) for a public school in Vancouver, WA.
Photo: Tom Collicott.

2-14
Formica laminate inlay (detail) from Tommy's Diner, Middletown, RI.
Photo: R. J. S. Gutman.

2-15
In Formica We Trust (detail).
A2Z's monumental ColorCore necklace designed for the installation of "Surface and Edge," an exhibition of ColorCore jewelry at the Pacific Design Center's WestWeek design market, 1986, in Los Angeles.
Photo: Levon Parian.

the surfaces of ivory and tortoiseshell, those materials that celluloid also substantively replaced. Early molders of Bakelite approximated wood grain by swirling together brown, black, and dark red. Polyurethane foam now captures the surface texture and color of rock as easily as of wood, and the fiber glass–polyester façades of Disney World mimic the material surfaces of all history. Nothing embodies this pride in the ingenuity of imitation more than Formica laminate, with its marbles, pearls, granites, linens, and, of course, wood grains. With the revival of fifties' design motifs, Formica laminate now even imitates itself.

Unlike other plastics, however, Formica laminate has always retained a directness, an element of sincerity, in its imitation of other surfaces. The dark line of its phenolic core appears strong and clear at every edge or corner. No matter how convincing the complex butcher-block patterning of a Formica laminate-surfaced coffee table, those dark brown lines expose the illusion and invite us to admire its cleverness. In 1982 all of this changed when Formica Corporation introduced ColorCore, a "revolutionary" laminate that eliminated the telltale edge line. A sheet of ColorCore is the same color throughout; as a recent sales booklet announces, it "offers the illusion of volume where surface planes meet." [10] In other words, a wooden cube surfaced with ColorCore looks like a solid cube of artificial material. Ironically, just as many designers are embracing such traditional imitative strategies as *faux* marble, it has become possible to simulate solid masses of frankly artificial plastic with ColorCore, a solid laminate material available in more than 115 colors. The

55

essence of Formica laminate, its frankly imitative surface, has vanished. The ultimate surface material, while seeking solidity, has become surfaceless. In moving from surface flatness to an apparent solidity, plastic laminate has thus become insubstantial. The dramatic arrangement of untextured slabs of contrasting colors in flat, stylized, architectural silhouettes to which ColorCore lends itself in furniture and interiors seems but a momentary physical manifestation of the bold, simple, but unreal forms typical of computer animation. If plastic embodies a major cultural shift away from traditional reliance on a limited inventory of imperfect materials resistant to manipulation, and toward a desire for immediate control over a wide array of predictably certain materials, then Formica laminate's history is emblematic of that shift. Both substance and surface vanish in the attempt to realize an idealized, and therefore artificial, landscape.

2-16
A transhistorical, fiber glass, and polyester façade at Walt Disney World near Orlando, Florida. Plastics have become the means by which any surface effect is achieved. *Photo courtesy of Jeffrey L. Meikle.*

2-17
Interior designer Charles Morris Mount's upscale McDonald's on Manhattan's chic 57th street, built in the late 1980s. The ColorCore product was one of many materials used to create this grand fast-food restaurant. *Photo: Norman McGrath.*

Notes

1 Roland Barthes, *Mythologies*, trans. Annette Lavers (New York: Hill and Wang, 1972), 99. The quoted phrase is a paraphrase of Raymond Loewy from "Streamlining—It's Changing the Look of Everything," *Creative Design* 1 (Spring 1935), 22.

2 On natural plastics and celluloid see Robert Friedel, *Pioneer Plastic: The Making and Selling of Celluloid* (Madison: University of Wisconsin Press, 1983). For Baekeland's motivation, see his laboratory notebook BKL/I/1907, Baekeland Collection, Archive Center, National Museum of American History, Smithsonian Institution, Washington, D.C.

3 Diary quotations are from Diary 1 (December 9, 1907) and Diary 2 (January 23, March 25, July 15, 1908) in Series 8, Box 1. Baekeland first used the spelling "Bakalite." Skinner saw the article "Bakelite, a Condensation Product of Phenols and Formaldehyde, and Its Uses," *The Journal of the Franklin Institute* 169 (January 1910), 55–60. Skinner's account of his association with Baekeland is reprinted in J. Harry DuBois, *Plastics History U.S.A.* (Boston: Cahners, 1972), 370–72. Baekeland recorded his visit in Diary 7 (June 9, 1910) in Series 8, Box 2. Celine Baekeland, who handled her husband's accounts in the early days, kept a ledger for "Orders" from February 12, 1908, to March 15, 1911. The anonymous associate's memories of Baekeland appear in "The Bakelite Story and Dr. Baekeland," an unpublished ms., Collection Division VI, Box 12, Folder VI-C-6. All manuscript sources are in the Baekeland Collection.

4 General information about Formica laminate here and below comes from Ward Moore, "Big Industry Built on Vision and Few Thousand Dollars," *Cincinnati Post*, 15 August, 1940, 19; "Formica Is on Top," *Fortune* 44 (October 1951), 116–18, 150, 154, 156; Formica Foremen's Business Club, "This Is Your Life: Mr. D. J. O'Conor" (75 pp. typescript), June 1, 1955; an interview with O'Conor conducted by William T. Cruse, February 22 [1968?], Plastics Pioneers Association Tapes, Reel 2, Side 2, National Museum of American History; and the pamphlet *Historical Growth of High Pressure Decorative Laminates* (Wayne, N.J.: Formica Corporation, ca. 1980). Specific details are from R. E. W. Moore, "Properties and Uses of Bakelite Micarta," *The* [Westinghouse] *Electric Journal* 10 (July 1913), 645–50; Baekeland, Diary 32 (September 19, 1921), uncat., National Museum of American History. "Bakelite-Dilecto—A New Insulating Material," *Electrical Review and Western Electrician* 68 (March 11, 1916), 479–80; "Bakelite-Micarta-D Gears and Pinions," *Electrical Review and Western Electrician* 69 (October 14, 1916), 693–94; and "New Material for Gears," *Industrial Management* 54 (October 1917), 118–21.

5 Sales figures are from "Formica Is on Top," 150. Edwin M. Wolcott's memories appeared in "This Is Your Life: Mr. D. J. O'Conor," 15.

6 "Bakelite Desk Tops," *Bakelite Information* #2 (April 1927), 1; "The Guest Room Up-to-Date," *Plastic and Molded Products* 3 (July 1927), 362; James L. Rodgers, "Plaskon, A New Molding Compound the Result of Planned Research," *Plastics and Molded Products* 7 (December 1931), 664–65, 687; and David A. Hanks with Jennifer Toher, *Donald Deskey: Decorative Designs and Interiors* (New York: E. P. Dutton, 1987), esp. 44–48, 108. Deskey probably used Westinghouse's Micarta in his interior design work, the most notable being Radio City Music Hall (1932).

7 O'Conor made this remark when interviewed by William T. Cruse, February 22 [1968?].

8 "Formica Is on Top," 116. See also "What's New in Decorative Laminates," *Modern Plastics* 28 (October 1950), 73–79; Belle Kogan, "Changing the Kitchen Scene," *Modern Plastics* 29 (March 1952), 104–5, 202, 205. On popular design of the 1950s and 1960s see Thomas Hine, *Populuxe* (New York: Knopf, 1986).

9 The major limit to this liberation, an ultimate one, is Earth's tolerance for chemical and solid wastes.

10 *Applied Designs: Formica Corporation Innovations* (Cincinnati: Formica Corporation, 1988), 15. This publication also has good illustrations of ColorCore interiors. For illustrations of furniture see Judy Coady, Susan Grant Lewin, Peggy A. Loar, and Bernice Wollman, *Material Evidence: New Color Techniques in Handmade Furniture* (Washington, D.C.: Smithsonian, 1985).

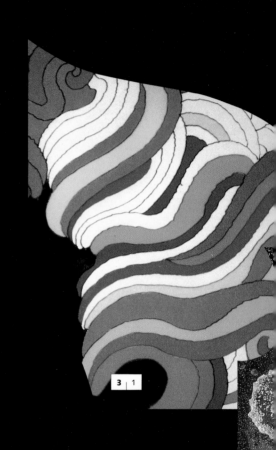

3 | 1

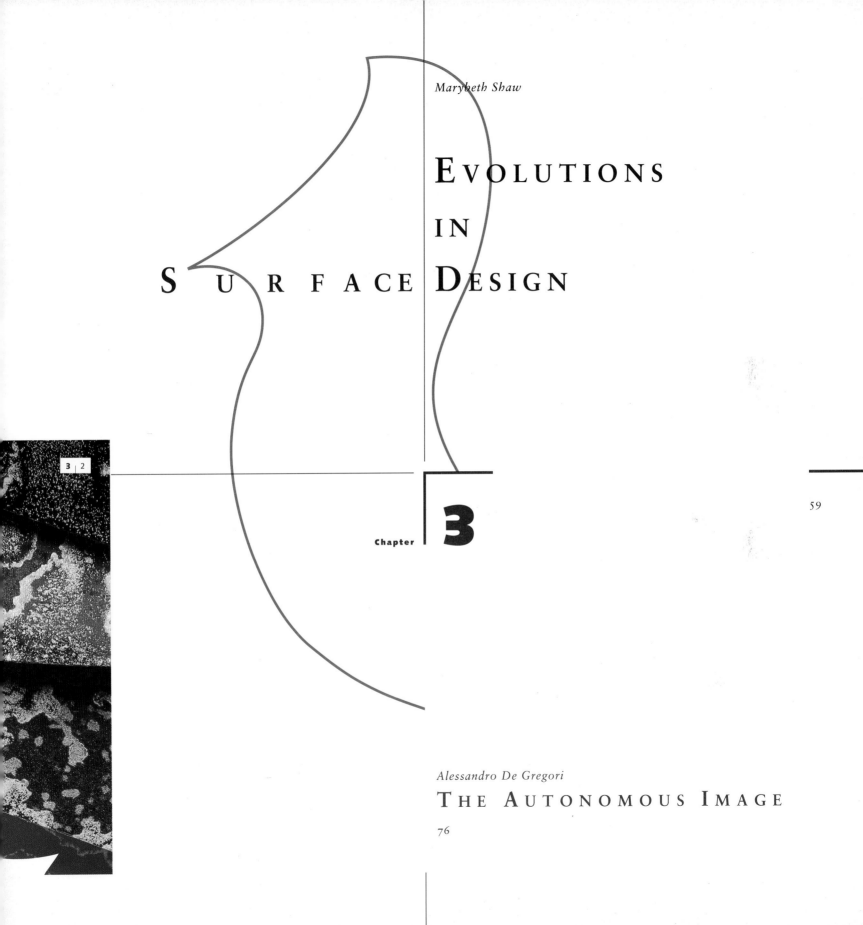

Marybeth Shaw

EVOLUTIONS IN SURFACE DESIGN

Chapter 3

3 | 2

Alessandro De Gregori

THE AUTONOMOUS IMAGE

76

In the twentieth century, materials invention and advanced production and communication processes have fostered the development of an international design network that diffuses notions of style and fashion and works to bring changes to the public awareness. New materials and their potential variations inspire creative minds, newly devised applications generate a demand for increased manufacturing and distribution, and the new style is readily absorbed into the marketplace. It is difficult to discern which force—designer, manufacturer, or public—is actually fueling the evolution of style. The compulsion to change and develop at an unprecedented rate is a function of the modern world.

3 | 3

3-1
In Bob Dylan (detail), 1966, Milton Glaser captured a sixties icon. The bright swirls of Dylan's hair expressed the spirit of the decade—youthful energy and optimism. *Photo: Milton Glaser, © 1966.*

3-2
Lacque Metallique patterns from Formica Corporation's European Editions collection, introduced to the American market in 1990.

3-3
The Design Concepts Collection was developed for application in high-end retail and commercial environments and offered graphic and textured laminate surfaces.

3-4
Formica laminate colors were reorganized in the early 1980s with The Color Grid. It included 72 colors that could be mixed and matched easily.

A retrospective glance at interior design in this century indicates rapidly shifting popular preferences. The ever-evolving array of colors and patterns pressed and preserved in Formica brand laminate is a particularly appropriate barometer of stylistic change because Formica laminate is certainly one of the quintessential interior design materials of this century. A plastic building material that has revolutionized the interior landscapes of our homes, commercial establishments, and institutions, it has also reflected the

3 | 4

3 5

3 6

3 8

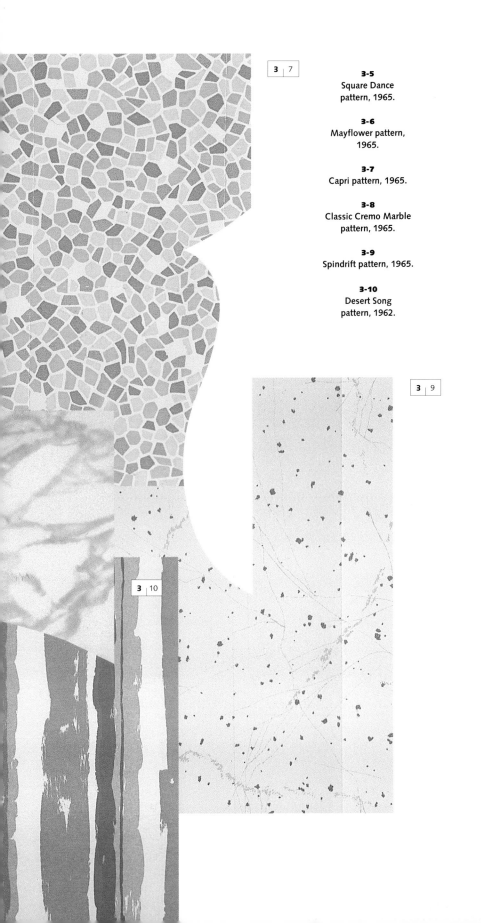

3 | 7

3-5
Square Dance
pattern, 1965.

3-6
Mayflower pattern,
1965.

3-7
Capri pattern, 1965.

3-8
Classic Cremo Marble
pattern, 1965.

3-9
Spindrift pattern, 1965.

3-10
Desert Song
pattern, 1962.

3 | 9

3 | 10

transformation and recurrence of colors and patterns in time. And colors and patterns, as we will see, correspond to societal moods and movements and provide an additional dimension to the history of popular culture.

By 1927 the first Formica brand laminate, composed of layers of kraft paper and topped with a solid black decorative sheet, was produced and sold to furniture manufacturers. The development of a urea-based resin in the early 1930s enabled The Formica Insulation Company to experiment with surface color and pattern for its sheet products. Early technological limitations, coupled with a depression-era longing for luxurious shades, motifs, and finishes, determined the look of the first series of laminate designs. Their prosperous, established values contrast starkly with our records of the monochromatic social and economic conditions of the decade.

In reaction, perhaps, to the "advances" of the machine age and the unbridled chaos of the financial collapse of the thirties, the Formica Company's reassuring early laminates drew upon nature and fine art for inspiration. Deep wood grains and leatherlike patterns in rich shades of brown and burgundy were photographically reproduced and colored. (No names were given to early laminate samples.) A cracked, stonelike pattern, similar to a crazed effect, was available in black with olive-green striations. One design, actually a linen fabric lamination, was decorated with a black floral and bird motif resembling early American decoration.

In a slightly brighter mode that responded to Art Deco influences, the company experimented with luxurious golden metallic effects in three amber-toned patterns, one of them a mosaic-

63

theme design. The other two were small- and large-scale organic designs suggestive of the microscopic world and swirling currents of liquid stone set against a black universe. The company also offered standard black laminate and developed methods for inlaying it with patterns in contrasting metal finishes well suited to the new skyscraper culture and to abstract geometric motifs.

Themes of sophistication and seriousness in the design of Formica laminate would last up to World War II when the company switched back to the exclusive production of materials for the war effort. In 1938, however, Matthew Luckiesh, an expert colorist and lighting designer, predicted a transition to brighter colors in the postwar era. In *Color and Colors,* he condemned the bleak tones of the thirties and encouraged the liberation of colors from the modern artist's canvas out into the daily living environment.[1] In essence, Luckiesh's color theory supported a democratization of color usage after the war that was fueled by Americans' optimistic consumption of variety and excess.

In the late 1940s, as the country regrouped and set its sights on the future, The Formica Company returned to manufacturing decorative laminate. In its design and marketing, the company did not distinguish between commercial and residential applications. The office of the postwar era drifted away from its factorylike division of labor design toward a homier, more comfortable atmosphere. Its colors were largely residential.

The Color Range, introduced in 1949,

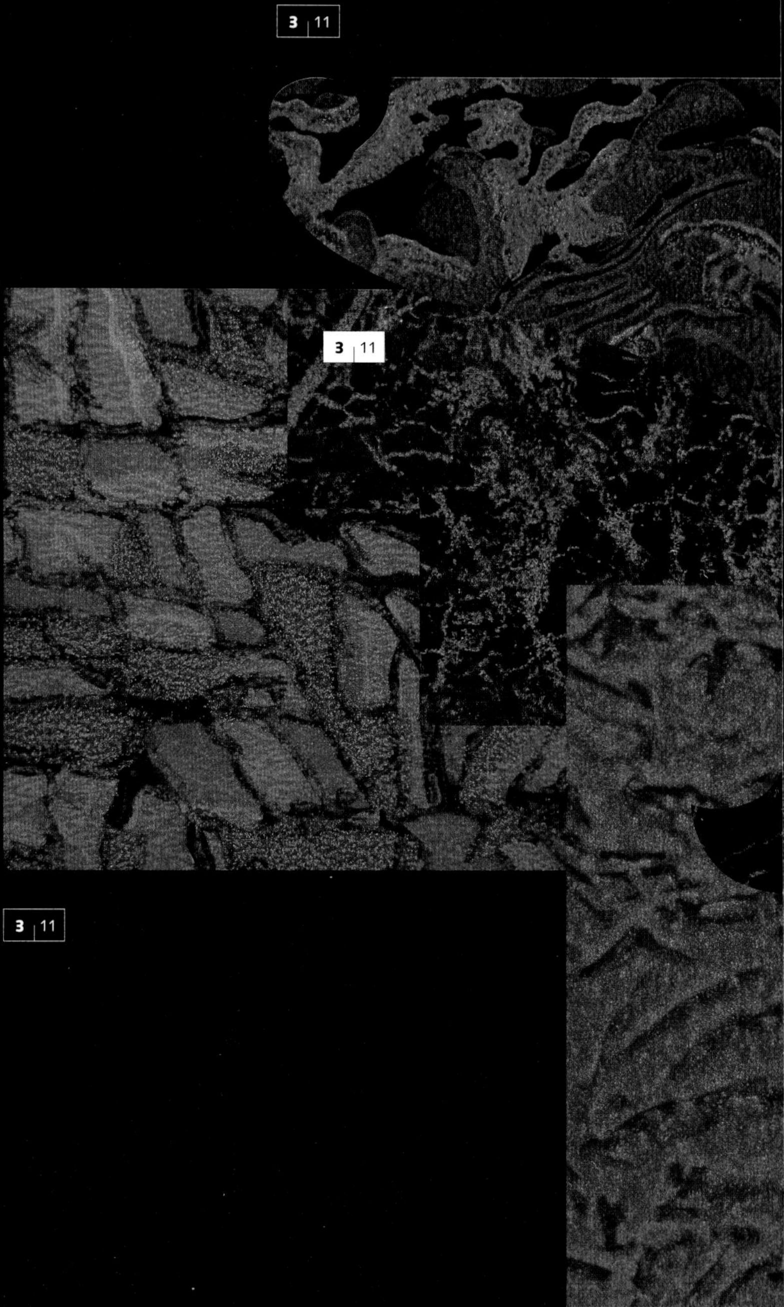

3 | 11

3 | 11

3 | 11

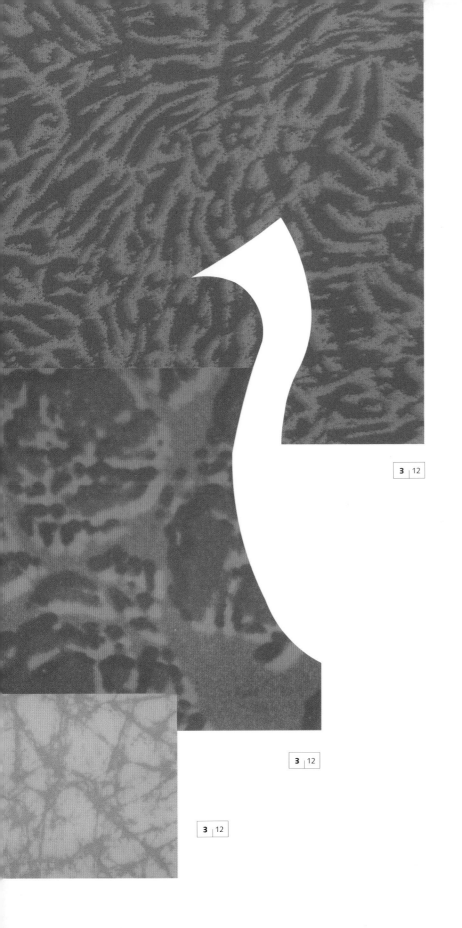

3 | 12

3 | 12

3 | 12

65

"available in both standard and cigarette-proof grades . . . in satin or polished finishes." The colors were comprised of pastel shades and muted brights. With the exception of Linen and Wood Finish, the patterns were upbeat, blatantly synthetic designs with a whimsical bent. Moonglo capitalized on Americans' fascination with outer space and futuristic themes. Pearl—originally created in the late 1930s—returned as a luminous best seller, with a modernized color offering. Arabesque and Batik were tone-on-tone patterns that heightened surface complexity. For its time, the vast and polychromatic nature of The Color Range was novel.

Concurrently, the influence of industrial design on American life was increasing. The public began to have access to trends in the fine arts and design in museums of modern and contemporary art, and industrial designers responded to the population's demands for "newness." In 1953 The Formica Company commissioned Raymond Loewy Associates to revise and revitalize its color line. Franz Wagner, Vice-President of Raymond Loewy Associates, wrote in 1954:

> Few products have as many and varied uses for so many people or so many potential applications. . . . Color and Formica are inseparable. . . . We have found that color makes the first impact on a customer, and pattern the second. Therefore, we based the new Formica color line, to be called the Formica Sunrise line, on a further-known fact about color's importance—that consumers should be offered a wide range of patterns in each of the more popular colors. We devised a Formica color system consisting of individual colors that are compatible with one another and with other colors likely to be used in the home or elsewhere. The exception to this color system is the line of high-style decorator colors.[2]

Thus, the distinction between the needs of the consumer and those of the professional designer was acknowledged and established as company design policy.

As a popular interpretation of abstract art; repeat patterns; and sculptural, organic, and asymmetrical forms, the Sunrise line evolved with the 1950s. The Skylark, Pearl, and Linen patterns were recolored, and new geometrics were introduced: Capri, an irregular mosaic; and Nassau, a soft geometric of overlapping translucent tones. Both were single tones of varying intensities on a neutral background. Raymond Loewy Associates also designed Milano, a close, mottled *faux* Italian marble in pink, yellow, black, and gray. Seventeen solid colors provided a bolder palette from which designers could select, including such colors as Citron and Pumpkin. Nineteen wood grains attested to that texture's consistent

popularity. While Picwood was a printed grain, Realwood offered natural grain by lamination of a genuine wood veneer.

The overlapping geometry and tone-on-tone styling of the patterns indicate a restrained suggestion of multiple colors. Only the celebrated Skylark design of 1950 integrated contrasting color outlines against solid bright and neutral backgrounds. Its curvilinear boomerangs dancing in color are a fitting summation of the lively, quirky designs of the 1950s. Skylark was used to surface equally curvaceous coffee tables, as well as soda fountains, counter tops, and restaurants across America.

Despite the unprecedented quantity and variety of consumer goods released to the market during the 1950s, the era also fostered a consolidation of American popular culture, values, and dreams. Many of the ethnically diverse immigrants were now grandparents with fully assimilated grandchildren. Televisions, cars, appliances, and easy-to-clean Formica laminate counter tops became the material yardsticks by which the younger generation measured its success, happiness, and relative well-being.

In industrial design, this uniformity was manifested in common-denominator design. In 1959 *This Formica World*, the company's quarterly magazine, published an article on patterns in which the company philosophy of the day, and that of Raymond Loewy Associates, was expounded: "Loewy's approach to new design is to create patterns which have as broad a base as possible in use." Formica Corporation's selection process was described as follows:

In determining which of the 72 colors and patterns remain in the Formica Sunrise Color Line and which are to be dropped, a constant check is made of the sales. A particular pattern's percent of sales is checked against the percent of sales of other patterns. . . . The fault often lies with choice of color. . . . In general, soft colors, both solids and patterns, are the best sellers. . . . Formica, being a durable product, is usually purchased in a "durable" color.[3]

The Nassau pattern, for example, first available in Sunshine Yellow, Sky Blue, Tropical Green, and Calypso Red, accounted for less than 1 percent of sales for the first six months of 1958. These four colorways were discontinued and three of them were lightened to neutral pastels. By November 1958 Sea Mist, Honey Beige, and Cameo were running at 32 percent of sales and gaining.[4]

Whether Formica Corporation's design determinations demonstrated good business sense or accommodation to the masses is a matter of perception. In order to remain competitive, the company had to strike a difficult balance between progressive design and market reality. It maintained its position by offering a limited spectrum of "designer" options in addition to neutral standards. In any case, the popularity of neutrals and pastels was about to suffer a dramatic upheaval as the mid-sixties approached and American society exploded in polychromatic color in all its anarchic, psychedelic brilliance.

Following the assassination of President Kennedy and in the midst of civil rights marches, Vietnam War protests, the women's rights movement, and experimentation with hallucinogenic drugs, the country seemed to erupt visually in bright, intense colors used all at once. The public eye finally opened to the colors of Jackson Pollock, Andy Warhol, and Roy Lichtenstein. The graphics of rock-concert posters and Milton Glaser reinforced the youthful identification with color.

Formica Corporation introduced a veritable spectrum of new colors in 1964— the Citation Series, which won an A.I.D. International Design Award and trumpeted the change. The series included such colors as Grape, Raspberry, Signal Red, Bittersweet, Lemon Twist, Lime, and Caribbean Blue. To round out the line, it offered more than thirty wood grains—from Spanish Oak to Snowgrain. These wood grains, together with several *faux* marbles, maintained their popularity through the early 1970s and underscored the public's acceptance of synthetic finishes imitating nature.

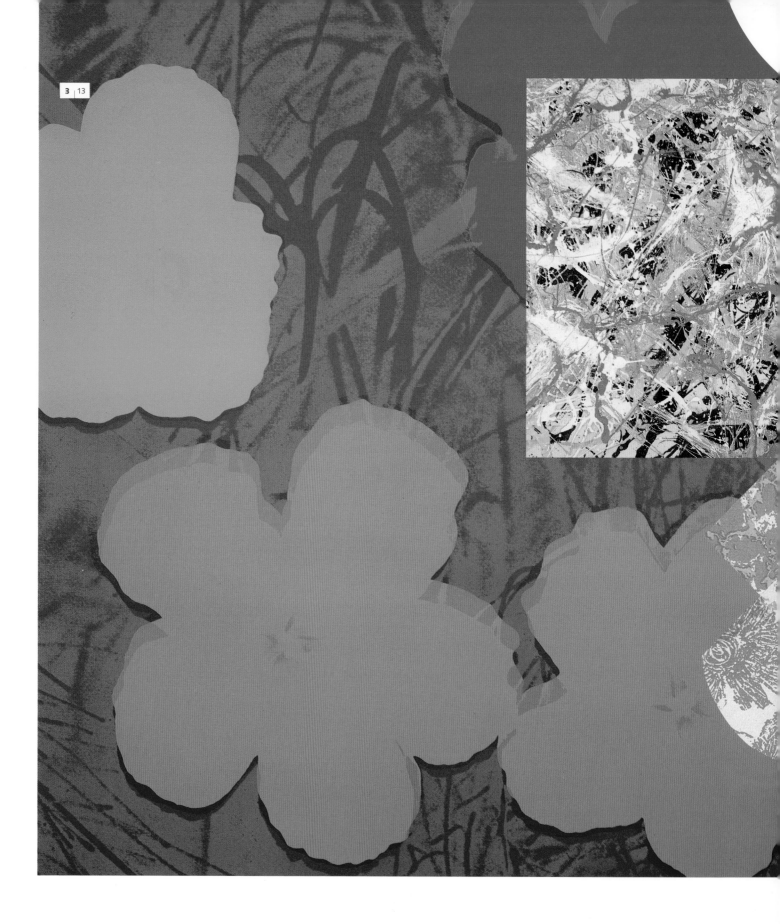

3-13
Andy Warhol, Flowers
(detail), 1970.
Warhol's silk-screen
canvases, with their
jarring colors, conveyed
both excitement
and cynicism.
*Photo courtesy of
Whitney Museum
of American Art.*

3-14
Jackson Pollock,
Number 27
(detail), 1950.
The chaotic energy of
abstract expressionism
was introduced to
the American public
in the 1950s.
*Photo courtesy of
Whitney Museum
of American Art.*

3-15
Opaline pattern, 1965.

3-16
Garland pattern, 1965.

In addition, Formica Corporation kept nine patterns that seemed to be holdovers from the late 1950s. They were characterized by organic-looking repeat designs in tone-on-tone pastel colors, similar to the wrapping-paper designs Warhol created in the 1950s. Linen remained in the line, as did the Sequin pattern, updated with random sketch lines and renamed Spindrift. Nassau evolved into the looser, fossil-like patterns, Beige and Gray Frost. Such a dramatic rift in the product offering between bright solid colors and soft, diluted patterns may have reflected the era's confusion and splits on social and political issues, as well as the newly labeled "generation gap."

One provision for the commercial designer was Formica Special Designs "for a dramatic change of pace in surface treatment . . . for controlled emphasis." A series of thirty-two silk-screen patterns and motifs, ranging from Montezuma to Virginia Reel, could be specified in any color combination and superimposed on a background of solid-color, patterned, or wood-grain laminate of the customer's choice. Seeing was believing these overpowering designs installed as wall panels in "Spanish Mediterranean," "French provincial," and "contemporary" interiors of the late 1960s. The company abandoned its silk-screening process in 1969, however. Plans to expand custom business and specialty products, which include reintroduction of the silk-screening process, are in research and development.

By the early 1970s, the era of Sliced Avocado and Harvest Gold had arrived, indicating a renewed restraint in color and mood. The National Housewares Manufacturers Association survey of 1971

69

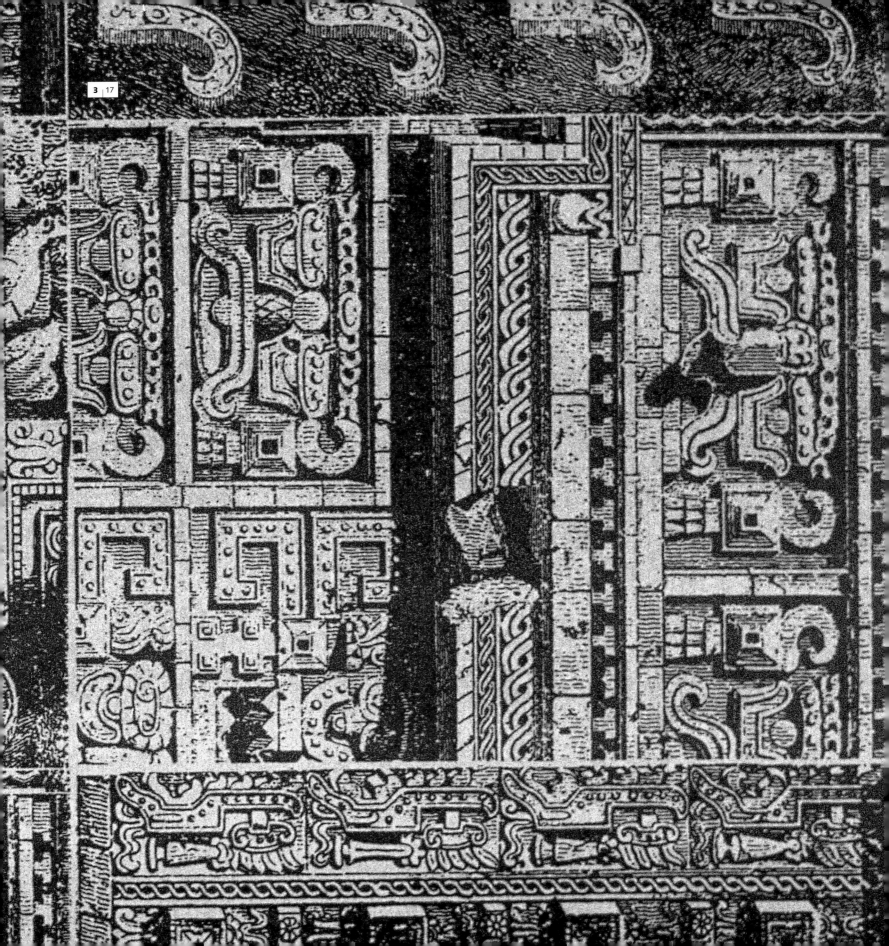

ranked Avocado as the most popular color choice for 1972 in four separate housewares accessories categories, with Harvest Gold gaining strength.[5] Formica Corporation's sales figures for the third quarter of 1971 echoed these findings. Right behind White, White Sequin, and Spanish Oak, the Avocado Gossamer and Gold Leather patterns ranked fourth and sixth, respectively.[6]

As the mid-1970s approached, a societal "need" prevailed for earth tones and variations on the "brown" theme. The political and social trauma of the immediate past, as well as a growing awareness of the environmental movement, led consumers to demand products that were true to nature. Brown, a color that was believed to promote nurturing and sincerity, appeared to be the remedy. Formica laminate lost a good deal of desirability because of its blatant plasticity. Natural materials—tile, real wood, macrame, and ferns—were perceived as more "dependable." Interestingly enough, the bright orange color, Bittersweet, remained popular as did certain bold, metallic finishes, perhaps indicative of the country's newly placed belief in computer technology as the hard-and-fast key to the future.

In retrospect, the 1970s are not noted for great design breakthroughs. The more modern, high-tech design themes that characterized the latter part of the decade were generally monochromatic. Solid white was the base upon which minute quantities of color, usually in the form of accessories, were gingerly applied. By 1981, however, a new neutral was the leading color in interior design: Almond. Gentle, always-appropriate Almond acted as a pillar of indecisiveness that paved the way for the

3-17
Montezuma pattern,
1962.

3-18
Barnwood pattern,
1966.

3-19
Paldao pattern, 1966.

3-20
Rosewood pattern,
1965.

3-21
Mondrian pattern, 1965.

3-22
Raintree pattern, 1962.

3 | 22

3 | 21

grayed pastel shades of the next decade's major design force: postmodernism.

In response to the increasing public awareness of design and designers, Formica Corporation had formed a Design Advisory Board (DAB) in the late 1970s to guide the company's product line in a more progressive direction. The first result was The Color Grid®, a systematic organization of seventy-two existing and new solid colors in Formica laminate, divided into neutral and chromatic categories. The Color Grid was adopted by Formica Corporation as a permanent offering that promised availability of these colors indefinitely. In a more flexible vein, Color Trends allowed for yearly changes in the popularity of approximately thirty postmodern pastel shades.

The DAB also developed the Design Concepts® collection of premium solid color, lacquer, and contrasting matte-patterned laminates that served a more "high design" commercial or retail style. In turning its attention toward designers, the company developed ColorCore surfacing material, a solid-color-throughout laminate that eliminated the dark seam at edges and allowed for volumetric illusions and custom fabrication details that the designers themselves explored. ColorCore was manufactured in all 108 solid colors of The Color Grid and Color Trends.

73

3 24

3 25

3 | 26

3 | 27

3 | 28

75

3 | 29

3-23
Nassau pattern, 1954.

3-24
Mantilla pattern, 1962.

3-25
Dutch Garden
pattern, 1962.

3-26
Sliced Avocado
pattern, 1972.

3-27
French Blue
pattern, 1972.

3-28
Adobe Gold
pattern, 1972.

3-29
Bittersweet pattern,
1972.

New York architect and former DAB
member Charles Boxenbaum has noted:

> Design Concepts was a breakthrough in the manipulation of an
> applied finishing material. Formica took advantage of the potential
> of its process to create a laminate that had a visual surface unique to
> its product. Like it or not, there is usually a compelling integrity to
> such materials. The ColorCore development, on the other hand, took
> an established product which was perceived in a particular and
> limited way, and made it what it really wanted to be. By eliminating
> the visual distinction between backing and surface, it encouraged us
> to see that this material had potential far beyond its previous realm
> of lamination for serviceability.[7]

All of these lines were solid-color
innovations that coincided with
postmodernism's reliance on simplified,
historic references in form—not pattern—

THE AUTONOMOUS IMAGE

*Laminates are a source of visual and
tactile invention that constantly propose
surface design issues. A compelling issue
voiced by architects and interior designers
is that of the "integrity" of a material. This
issue implies that a surfacing material
should express its own identity, functional
characteristics, aesthetic quality, and
ability to communicate a cultural message.
Synthetic surfaces simulating the
appearances of natural materials have
often been neglected by this group. Wood
reproductions in laminates, for instance,
are sometimes considered a distorted form*

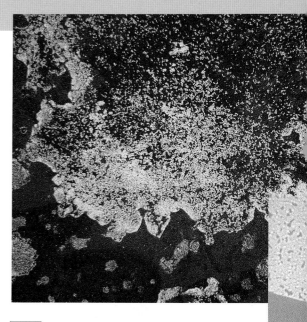

3 | 30

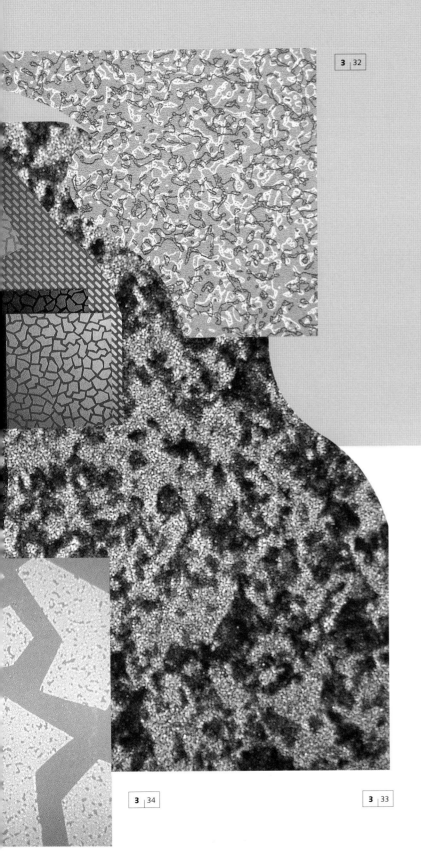

3-30
Patina Lacque
Metallique
pattern, 1990.

3-31
Design Concepts
Collection
2 patterns, 1988.

3-32
Ninja Crimble
pattern, 1990.

3-33
Gray Stone Galaxia
pattern, 1990.

3-34
Slate Rock
pattern, 1988.

of communication, and are therefore devalued.

In a popular and utilitarian context, however, the familiarity and natural comfort of the image of wood has a value and identity somewhat independent of its material carrier even when—as in the case of laminates—the carrier of the image is printed paper.

Interestingly, designers have accepted and popularized laminate reproductions of wood-grain patterns that are tinted or painted in fashionable colors; cultural attitudes toward decoration change over time. This suggests that the issue of the material's integrity may be negotiable at all cultural levels, as long as semantic and aesthetic priorities are met. What seems to have been accepted in the case of the colored wood grains is the priority of color

77

for ornament. Surface colors remained milky and monochromatic. Texture was largely left unaddressed in interior designs that stressed planar, façadelike motifs.

By the mid-1980s, popular design also began to reflect the impact of the bright and liberating design group Memphis. This international consortium of architectural, interior, furniture, and industrial designers, based in Milan, promoted new juxtapositions in volume, form, color, pattern, texture, and material. They discarded convention for invention and exploited high-pressure laminate's potential for versatility and complexity in surface color and pattern. Ettore Sottsass, Memphis's director, worked with Abet Laminati, an Italian laminate company and

and graphic manipulation over the fidelity of the pattern. As long as the coloration is right for the intended use of the material, the underlying pattern is considered appropriate. Because the "object of desire"—a representation of nature—is not playing a central role in the visual composition of the image, as it is in natural color reproductions, it is more widely accepted.

As images of natural materials become less important, the original issue of the integrity of the material is debased, as the whole inventory of images, new and reedited, traditional and contemporary, becomes autonomous with respect to the medium of the carrier. The new "optical solids," minute, pointillist formations that appear to be solid colors from a distance, provide another example of autonomous image. They are globally accepted by all orders of users and designers for different surfacing materials.

The concept of the autonomous image, then, allows a unified structural framework for a pattern language that is renewable and capable of narrative in visual compositions. This true and most challenging research for design begins by creating products that carry meaningful images and cultural references on their surface, enriching compositions of materials, objects, and spaces. Research at Formica Corporation has resulted in Formations, a comprehensive open system of solid colors coordinated with dimensional gradations of abstract patterns on laminates. The narrative in this case is the message of aging versus timelessness that is communicated by the

3 | 36

3 | 38

one of Formica's strongest European competitors, to create a series of provocative patterns in stunning colors that stirred American manufacturers to more innovative designs.

In 1986 and 1987 Formica Corporation launched a series of patterns that addressed the substantial gaps in its pattern offerings of recent years. Dust, Stripes, and Lacque Metallique, followed by Clear Sand, American Granite, and Papercraft, updated the line by two approaches: one reminiscent of 1950s' designs; and one that reconsidered, on a deeper level, the concept of surface. Papercraft, for instance, resembles finely handcrafted Italian paper, an amusing twist considering the fact that high-pressure laminate is made of paper.

3-35
Copper Maple Leaves
pattern, 1990.

3-36
Nacre Apricot
pattern, 1990.

3-37
Grecian Blue
Boomerang
pattern, 1988.

3-38
Patina patterns,
Formations
Collection, 1991.

3-39
Aluminum Mottle
pattern, 1990.

3-40
Faux Marble Padoue
pattern, 1990.

3 | 35

interaction of elements and materials with naturalistic references to pattern, color, and scale. This integration of scale with pattern and color was an industry first. Formations leads as a design model for the development of a pattern language capable of renewing the communicative power of the surface for today's pluralistic environment.

Alessandro De Gregori

3 | 39   3 | 40

79

The company updated the Design Concepts collection in 1988 with Flip and Rock—a response to the whimsical motifs of the Memphis movement. It also reintroduced the ever-popular Skylark pattern, renamed Boomerang. These pattern-oriented product launches have continued to the present day.

The 1980s demonstrated a remarkable pluralism of design doctrines—postmodernism, Memphis, neomodernism, deconstructivism—and a merciless pace to their accompanying stylistic changes. Colors seemed to have ever-shorter life spans in the popular palette. White, almond, gray, pastels, Day-Glos, and black focused our attention, one after another and in unison. As the decade concluded, brighter, white-based, saturated colors returned, and Formica Corporation again reorganized and revitalized its solid-color line to survive this evolution. The flexible, new Color + Color system divides the more than 100 colors by family, brightness, and value. To meet the design demand for texture, the company offers each color in seven different options, including matte, polished, leatherlike, and stonelike finishes. Despite popular trends, however, the company's sales statistics for 1989 reflected a preference for the standards: White, Almond, Folkstone (gray), and Black were ranked first through fourth in solid-color volume sales.[8]

The theme of collage plays a tremendous role in today's design and promotes freedom in mixing materials. Increasing the selection of materials for their lustrous, dimensional qualities and dialogues in the scale of texture and pattern are paramount concerns. Formica Corporation's most recent product releases—Formations™, a series of six abstracted organic designs in various scales; European Editions, a collection of lacquer, crimble (small-scale, organic motif), and painted wood designs in a wide range of colors; and the International Collection of Formica brand Metal Laminates, mirrored, brushed, and embossed designs in a variety of metallic tones—support this focus and emphasize the company's commitment to exploiting its internationally integrated research, design, and distribution.

Color is certain to continue to evolve on increasingly universal terms as the international design community sets global standards. With respect to this short-term forecast, Formica laminate should be capable of growing in value as a versatile design product.

The coming years will, most likely, see a refinement and consolidation of the numerous design trends of the 1980s, and, if the company so deems, it can increase the scope and depth of Formica laminate's visual and tactile interest—something that Americans, educated by the international design community, desire. Formica Corporation's acknowledgment of the heightened design sophistication of consumers is tied directly to its business strategy. Vincent P. Langone, Chairman, President, and Chief Executive Officer, has stated, "Our corporate insurance policy for the future is tied directly to our dialogue with the global design community—and to our ability to listen and respond to its needs." With this determination to invoke new talent and ideas from around the world, Formica brand laminate should remain a popular—and multicultural—icon, all within the limitations of its low-tech, two-dimensional composition.

3-41
A sample chain of
F-chips and ruler, 1930s.

3-42
Granito pattern,
Formations Collection,
1991.

3-43
Patina pattern,
Formations Collection,
1991.

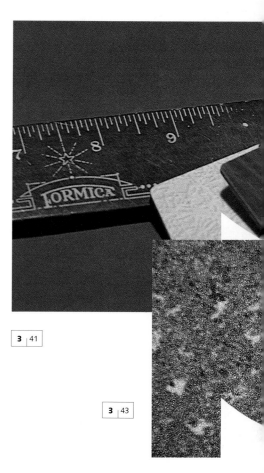

3 | 41

3 | 43

Notes

1   Matthew Luckiesh, *Color and Colors* (New York: Van Nostrand Co. Inc., 1938), 153–55.

2   Franz Wagner, "Color Makes the First Impact," *This Formica World* 6 (1954), 9–10.

3   Jack Alexander, "Patterns and How They Got That Way," *This Formica World* 10 (1959), 2-3.

4   Memo from R. T. MacAllister, Formica Corporation, to Jerry Graham, Perry Brown, Inc., November 14, 1958.

5   National Housewares Manufacturers Association Survey, 1971.

6   Memo from H. B. Shear, Formica Corporation, to All Sales Offices, Formica Corporation, "General Purpose Laminate Sales Analysis, 3rd Quarter 1971," December 9, 1971.

7   Charles Boxenbaum. Interview with author, May 1988 via telephone.

8   "Active Warehouse and Factory Sales Report," Formica Corporation, 1st Quarter 1989, April 7, 1989.

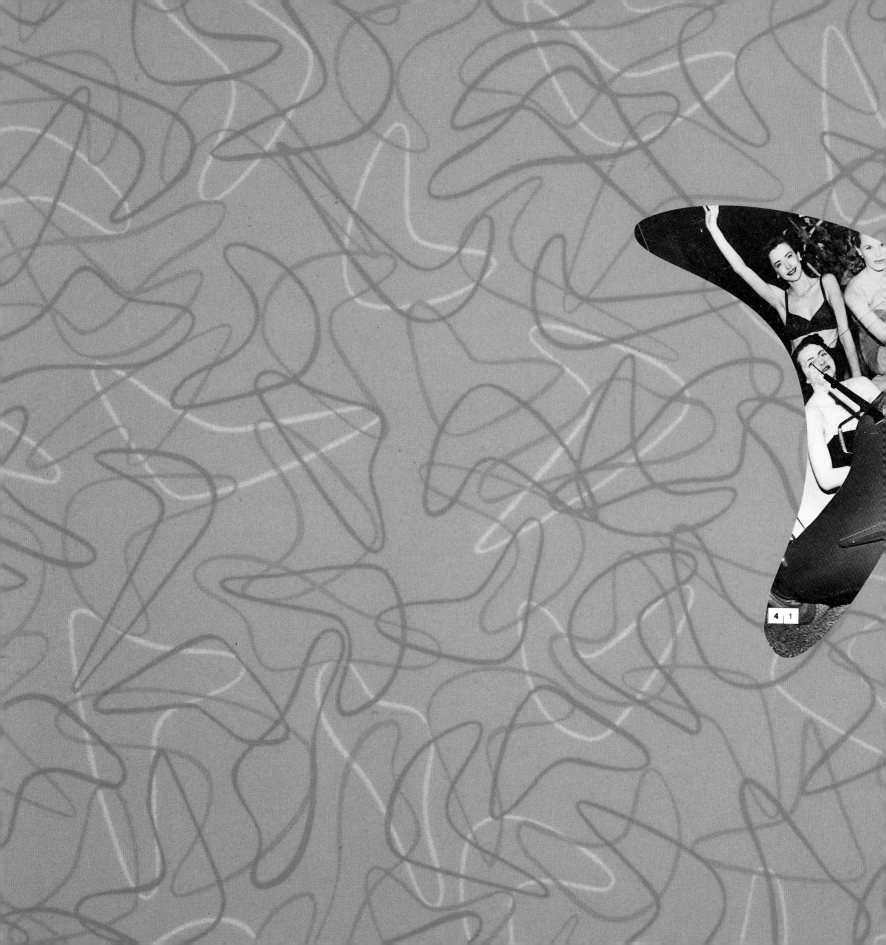

4 1

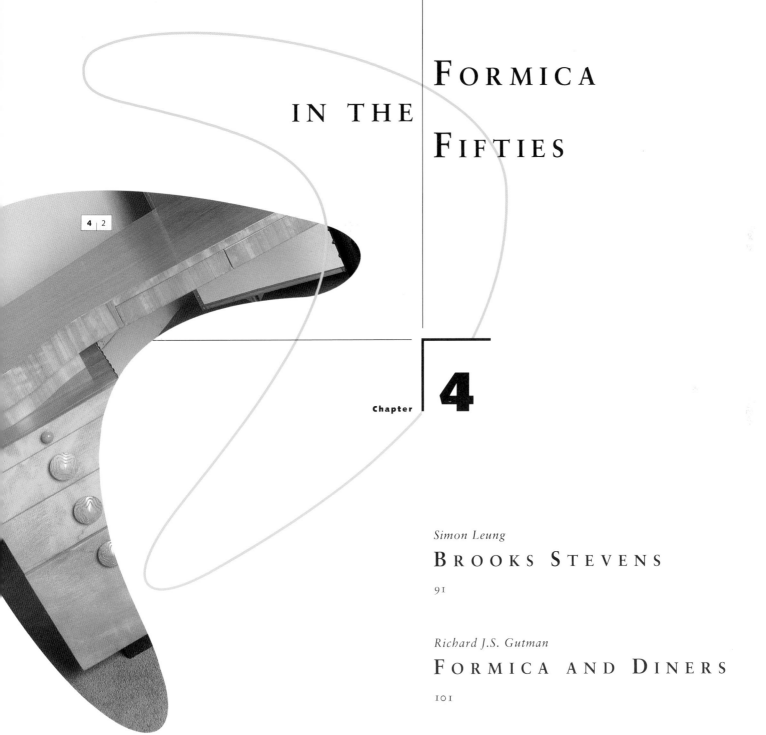

Barbara Goldstein

FORMICA
IN THE
FIFTIES

4 | 2

Chapter | **4**

Simon Leung

BROOKS STEVENS

91

Richard J.S. Gutman

FORMICA AND DINERS

101

In retrospect, the 1950s were more a state of mind than an actual decade. For the promoters of "good design," the fifties encompassed notions first developed in the late 1920s and realized in mass-produced objects until the early 1960s. To the catalogers of popular culture, the era began in the mid-1950s and extended to the middle of the next decade. Undoubtedly, however, whether one is examining good taste or popular culture, the force that bound the 1950s together was consumerism.

The 1950s were contradictory years. They began with an optimism about starting a new life after the last war, but this optimism was tempered by the threat of the Cold War. They were fueled by a desire for modernity but reined in by the political conformity of the McCarthy Era and the social conformity of suburban living. The era began with a shortage of material goods

4-1
A publicity shot introducing the "All-plastic Car," from the 1952 New York International Motor Show.

4-2
Organic, curvilinear shapes characterized the designs of the 1950s, foreshadowed in this 1938 Gilbert Rohde desk.
Photo courtesy of Fifty/50.

4-3
Veterans camped out overnight to sign up for suburban houses in Levittown, Long Island, New York, ca. 1947. William J. Levitt created suburban communities called "Levittowns" in New York (1947), Pennsylvania (1950), and New Jersey (1954).
Photo courtesy of Levittown Public Library.

4-4
Workers building "Levittown" houses during the postwar years.

4-5
A moment of "populuxe"—lush colors, luxury, and leisure.
Photo courtesy of New York Public Library.

85

and an oversupply of consumers and ended with an overabundance of consumer products and a mass acceptance of planned obsolescence.

It was a period of massive change, when the United States was recovering not only from material shortages necessitated by the war but from the poverty of the depression that preceded it. Immediately after the war, there was a severe housing shortage, and many young families were homeless, forced to live with relatives or in substandard dwellings. By 1944 the government had responded to the crisis by introducing the GI Bill, which offered veterans low-cost loans.

Housing developers like William J. Levitt became extremely inventive in their

4-6
The 1959 Cadillac Coupe De Ville was the epitome of fifties luxury cars. It also had the most elaborate tail fin of any Cadillac model produced before or since.
Photo courtesy of General Motors.

4-7
Eve Arnold, A Sailor Home on Leave (detail), 1953.
Photo courtesy of Magnum Photo.

4-8
This streamlined train from The Pennsylvania Railroad was designed by Raymond Loewy in the 1930s. Loewy, famous as an industrial designer, worked with Formica Corporation as a consultant in the 1950s.
Photo courtesy of Hagley Museum Archives.

4 | 8

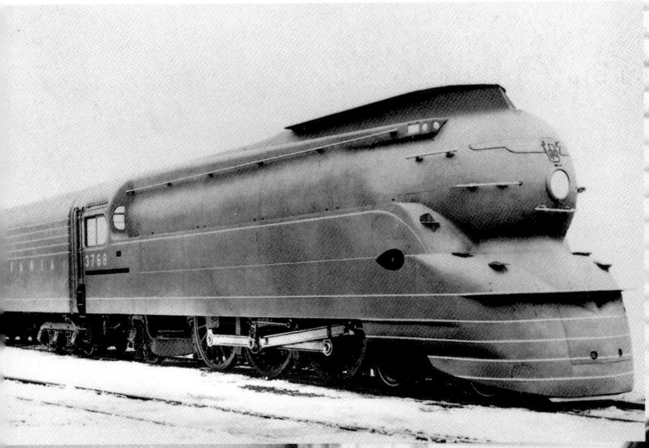

4 | 7

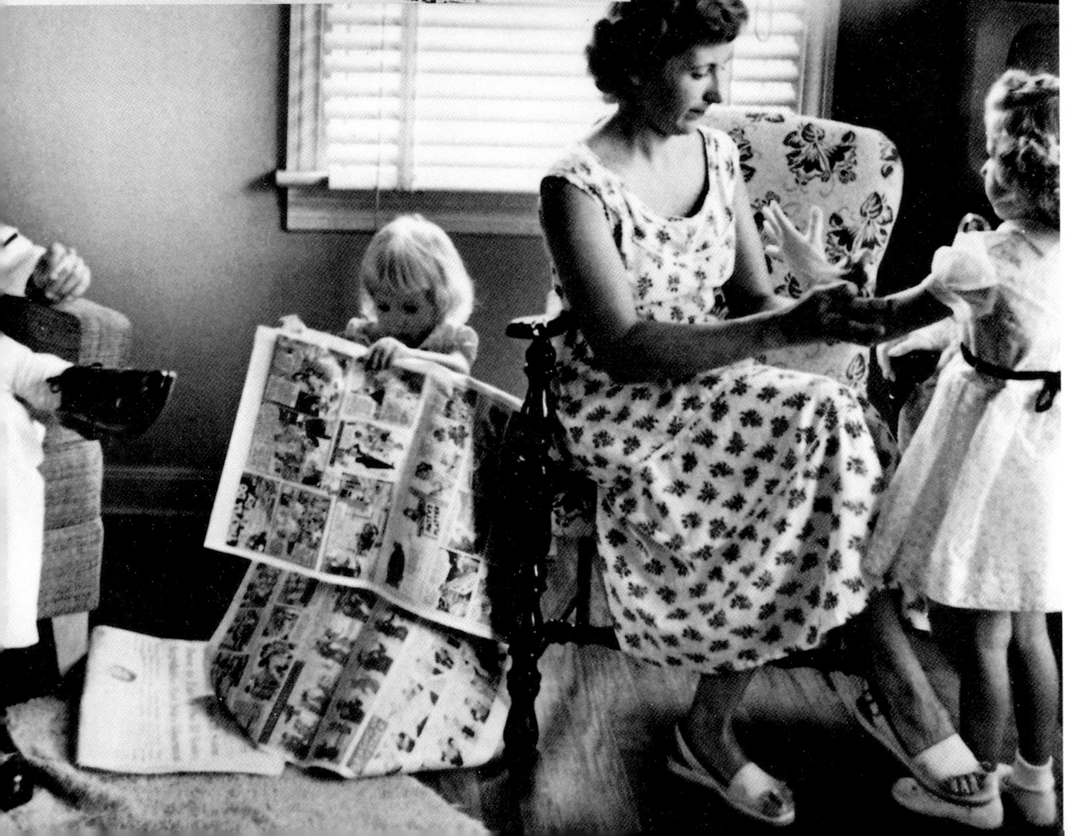

response to the demand for housing. They developed mass-produced housing that relied on an assembly-line approach: Workers would carry out one simple task, then move on to the next house. Materials like plastic laminates and asphalt-tile flooring predominated because they were easier to install and less expensive than their precursors—ceramic tile and hardwood floors.

A postwar tract house could be sold for less than $10,000. Levitt's first development, built in 1946 on a former Long Island potato field, consisted of hundreds of houses offered for $9,950. By 1947 he had coined the term "Levittown," was building 150 homes a week, and selling them for $6,900 each.[1] The uniformity of the new houses and the sterility of the suburbs were to have a tremendous impact on family structure and social patterns, contributing to the conformity of the era.

In the area of Good Design, John Entenza of *Arts & Architecture* magazine was promoting a different solution. He was convinced that, given encouragement, architects could produce innovative modern houses, using new and existing mass-produced materials in new ways. In 1945, he commissioned a group of idealistic designers, including Richard Neutra, Craig Ellwood, and Pierre Koenig, to design two-bedroom prototype houses for the postwar family. These houses were then fully furnished and opened to the public for view. While they were an inspiration to architects worldwide, and some of their design features entered the popular vocabulary, their modern style did not achieve mass acceptance.

Formica brand laminate responded perfectly to the postwar housing boom.

4 | 10

4 | 9

4-9
A 1950 advertisement photograph for the ''Vanitory.'' Formica laminate came to replace ceramic tile in American bathrooms in the 1950s.

4-10
The golden age of Formica.
A significant number of the six million kitchens built during the 1945–53 postwar suburban boom were specified in Formica brand laminate.

4-11
The display cases and paneling at Roeser's Bakery in Chicago were remodeled in 1954 using Frost Walnut Picwood Formica laminate.
Photo courtesy of John C. Roeser, III.

4-12
This Formica laminate advertisement photograph from the late 1940s features a powder room designed by Skidmore, Owings & Merrill Architects.

89

Easy to fabricate and less expensive than the materials it replaced, the laminate spanned both ends of the housing spectrum. While its design, color, and physical presence all signaled it as modern, its mass production and popular acceptance made it possible for everyone to conform to the same aesthetic standards. It kept pace with the colors and patterns dictated by fashion and, through its styling and marketing, carved an enormous niche for itself in the market. By the early 1950s, one-third of the new homes being built in America used laminate, much of it Formica.

Plastic laminate in the fifties was on the crest of a design wave. Because of its inherently ersatz qualities, its designers and manufacturers realized that it would be possible and, in fact, desirable to break entirely new aesthetic grounds, to experiment with color and pattern, and to invent uses for a previously nonexistent material. Sensing this, Formica Corporation promoted the material to fabricators, do-it-yourselfers, and architects. Formica hired Brooks Stevens and later Raymond Loewy as their design consultants and launched extensive advertising campaigns in publications ranging from *Life* magazine to *House Beautiful.* Formica laminate was promoted as a worry-free product for the housewife, desirable for its style as well as its wipe-clean, spill-proof surfaces. New uses were invented: Tabletops and modern furniture were surfaced with Formica laminate, and the product was widely used in the forward-looking design of airplanes, buses, restaurants, and diners.

The development of the product for domestic use found its perfect niche in the psychology of the 1950s: the return to the traditional notions of home and hearth. Perhaps in reaction to the war, women were transformed from their capable roles as workers in American industry to the "little ladies" managing the new "scientific" American kitchens. Open-plan suburban houses made the woman the pilot of the domestic ship, reinforcing this central role. As Betty Friedan noted in *The Feminine Mystique,* "There are no true walls or doors; the woman in the beautiful electronic kitchen is never separated from her children. . . . In what was basically one free-flowing room, instead of many rooms separated by walls and stairs, continual messes continually need picking up."[2] As an easy-to-clean, modern material, Formica laminate took its place in the live-in kitchen alongside the refrigerator and the range.

4-13
Can you spot the laminate surfaces?
Yes, that's Formica laminate on the end tables, but the cinder-block walls are also surfaced with Formica laminate sheets.

4-14
The Milwaukee Road, a locomotive designed by Brooks Stevens.

4-15
A miniature case designed for Herman Miller by George Nelson Associates in 1954. *Photo courtesy of Herman Miller Inc.*

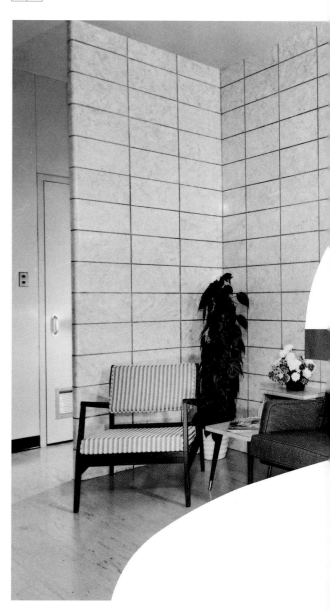

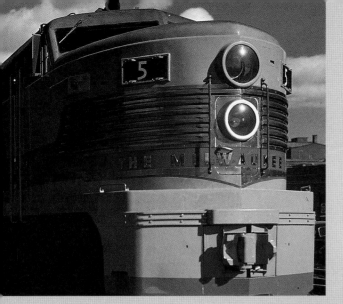

4 | 14

BROOKS STEVENS

Through the many successful competitions and museum exhibitions it has sponsored in the last decade, Formica Corporation has increasingly been identified with some of the most prominent architects and designers of this period. But the company's association with important designers of the day actually began almost half a century ago. Many are familiar with industrial designer Raymond Loewy's commissioned work for Formica in the mid-fifties, when his design team brought the company's color line into the "jet-age" with the Sunrise Collection, most notably with its updating of the colors for the classic Skylark pattern. But how many are aware of the contributions of Brooks Stevens, who in 1950 actually introduced Skylark?

4 | 15

The 1950s' suburban tract house was a trap to which consumers readily submitted, however, and Formica sales literature, like much of the advertising copy of the era, reinforced popular notions about the woman's role in society. Feminist concerns notwithstanding, the company's development was a triumph of marketing and design. A legion of sales materials was sent forth to fabricators, furniture manufacturers, and builders. The name Formica became pervasive and highly recognized.

Let's examine the evolution of Formica laminate from a retiring and utilitarian servant to an attention-grabbing fashion material that became a feature in every American home.

Although widely respected as one of the most important American industrial designers of the twentieth century, Brooks Stevens has remained somewhat obscure outside of the design profession. As one of the ten founding members of the Society of Industrial Designers (today called the Industrial Design Society of America), Stevens is not as well known as his fellow charter members Raymond Loewy, Henry Dreyfuss, and Walter Dorwin Teague. But the breadth and quality of his work, which included airplanes, appliances, and forty years of automobile design, ranging from the 1940 Packard to the 1980 A.M.C. Cherokee station wagon, have insured Brooks Stevens the distinction of being the last of the great industrial designers. Self-described as "a businessman, an engineer, a stylist—in that order,"[1] Stevens understood "the desire to own something a little newer and a little better, a little sooner than necessary,"[2] and coined the term planned obsolescence to describe this relationship designers and consumers have with a capitalist economy.

Stevens's work with Formica Corporation in the postwar years embodied this philosophy. In addition to introducing the futuristic Skylark pattern, Brooks Stevens & Associates worked with the developmental laboratories of Formica Corporation in the late forties to create Luxwood—the Formica wood-grain laminate that seems to have covered so much of the furniture of that era. Luxwood was a technological advance over the company's earlier wood grain, Realwood. Unlike Realwood, which was an actual

4 | 16

4 | 18

Design in the 1950s was born in the 1930s. The products of European Modernism, design ideas gestated during the war years were sprung upon the hungry American public as the GIs flooded back from the European and Asian theaters. As early as 1929, Gilbert Rohde designed the first unornamented bedroom set for the Herman Miller company. By 1939 Eero Saarinen and Charles Eames had won the Museum of Modern Art international design competition for modern chairs. By the mid-1940s, Herman Miller and Knoll International were in business designing entirely modern furniture. The Good Design Era, which had been restrained by the onset of World War II, was in full swing.

The Good Design Era was

flitch of wood in a laminate, Luxwood was a photographic reproduction of actual wood grains and was thus consistent in its coloration and impervious to nature's changing course—a great advantage when it came time to match an earlier installation with a later one. Another advantage was price: Luxwood, unlike Realwood, cost no more to produce than regular Formica laminates. Offered in colors ranging from light blond to dark red-brown, Luxwood opened completely new markets for Formica laminates.

At about the same time that he was working on Luxwood, Stevens undertook another project that became one of the most comprehensive and exemplary applications of Formica laminate in the history of the product. During the mid-1940s the Chicago, Milwaukee, and

93

4-16
Hot Dog To Go: a 1958 Wienermobile designed by Brooks Stevens for the Oscar Mayer Company.

4-17
Interior views of the Hiawatha lounge cars. Note the color-coordinated greens and earth tones.

4-18
The famous Eames Chair of 1946 embodied the "Good Design Era." It was modern, lightweight, and easy to assemble. *Photo courtesy of Fifty/50.*

characterized by natural woods and plywood used in an unadorned state; strong colors and interesting textures; lightness; bold free-form and geometric shapes; and unit design—storage cabinets and seating designs that could be assembled in various configurations. Many of these ideas were popularized after the war, and early Formica laminate was in tune with the austere purity of this period. Its product range consisted of muted primary colors, Realwood—a laminate that used actual wood veneer—Linen, and several subdued, vaguely organic patterns including Moonglo, Pearl, Fernglo, and Surfglo.

As the decade progressed, a new stratum of popular aesthetics grabbed

St. Paul Railroad commissioned Stevens to design ten complete railroad trains for a line running from Chicago to Minneapolis-St. Paul, and another from Chicago to Seattle. The results were the Twin Cities Hiawathas and the Olympian Hiawathas trains.

As the overall exterior and interior design consultant for the trains, Brooks Stevens & Associates was able to design the trains completely—everything from the locomotives to the passenger cars. Not confined to the standard Pullman-car configuration and cross sections, since the cars were to be custom-made in Milwaukee, Stevens was able to introduce many structural as well as design innovations, including a "strata-dome" lounge that allowed a panoptic view of the landscape and the skies.

4 | 19

public attention: images of the jet and atomic ages, brighter secondary colors, more extravagant styling. Good design was replaced in the American home by what Thomas Hine had dubbed *populuxe,* "the moment when America found a way of turning out fantasy on an assembly line."[3] In the populuxe era, bright colors, aerodynamic styling, and pure ostentation were celebrated by an endless parade of new consumer objects and trends: heavy furniture on spindly legs, cars with tail fins, boomerang-shaped furniture, and spike-heeled shoes.

In the early 1950s Formica laminate, a neutral synthetic material, straddled both worlds. With its solid colors and wood-grain finishes, it could be used in "good design"

4-19
Brooks Stevens,
ca. 1950.

4-20
1950s pattern.
Photo: Moyra Davey.

Concerned with choosing materials and color schemes that would be long-lived and remain in first-class condition, Stevens used Formica laminates throughout the interiors of the trains.

Virtually unlimited in range of color, resistant to marring and scratching, and synthetically manufactured, Formica laminates resonated with a forward-looking sense of efficiency that seemed perfect for this streamlined symbol of progress. But recognizing "an interesting and stimulating battle . . . between tradition, convention, and the 'new look'"[3] in designing the postwar train, Stevens offered neither a cold, trimmed Modernist atmosphere nor the "parlor-car luxury" of some prewar trains. Instead, the lounges of the Hiawathas were described by Stevens as "living rooms on wheels."[4]

Stevens strove to individualize each room as much as possible. The interior coach walls were paneled with gray green and Realwood Formica laminates. The hallways were paneled in a blond satinwood finish. The sleeping cars, with their wainscoting, vestibule walls, and berths, were surfaced with linen finish, walnut, and gray green laminate panels, respectively. In the buffet-lounges, the tabletops, counters, and seat backs were covered in solid colors and blond wood grains. The same surfaces were covered with Formica laminate in the full diners, the wall areas relieved by an inlaid diamond-shaped floral pattern.

The use of different Formica laminate patterns and colors to distinguish the character and atmosphere of different spaces was most strongly felt in the

4 | 20

layouts, but it also began to offer a complete range of more popular patterns: Skylark (the boomerang), Capri (an irregular geometric mosaic reminiscent of the paintings of Piet Mondrian), and Milano (a pattern based on Italian marble).

In 1954 Raymond Loewy Design Associates brought Formica laminate more clearly into the "populuxe" era. Commissioned to "revise and revitalize" the product's color range, the firm put Formica laminate into the vanguard of popular interior design. Over time, Raymond Loewy Design Associates moved the Formica laminate line almost entirely away from its subdued, murky palette into a brighter and more stylized line.

*contrasting men's and women's lounges.
The walls of the men's lounges were
surfaced in light Realwood paneling, and
hunting prints in three-dimensional satin-
silver beveled frames hung over red leather
chairs, echoing a "den-like masculinity of
the club."*[5] *To create a feminine
atmosphere for the women's lounges,
Stevens used pastel blue or gray green
paneling with delicate, French-floral-print
inlaid laminates for the upper walls, and
ivory for the vanity and lower wainscoting.
In this "gendering" of spaces with Formica
laminates, Stevens foresaw the material's
design usage in decades to come.*

*In retrospect, Brooks Stevens's work
with Formica laminates on the Hiawathas
involved the designing of some of the very
elements of the postwar American idea of
life. It was a practical style based on seeing*

So what were Americans doing with
Formica laminate during the 1950s? The
product found its greatest use in the
revolutionized kitchen, where it was
employed as a unifying element in the
center of the up-to-date house. Because
it was manufactured in easily cut sheets,
kitchen fabricators found it a practical
replacement for ceramic tile as the perfect
surface material for counter tops. Its
colorful, wipe-clean, fruit-acid-resistant
surface made it attractive to the busy
housewife.

Stylistically, the 1950s' kitchen was
characterized by a standard counter height
and appliances that were subordinated to
an overall streamlined appearance. In
contrast with earlier kitchens, in which

4-21
The observation car
of the Hiawatha.

4-22
The Gilbert Rohde desk
of 1938 with its 1950s
legacy, the Mesa Table
by Robsjohn-Gibbings.
*Photos courtesy
of Fifty/50.*

into the future in a time of prosperity and recovery, a recovery with longing for stability and the feeling of "home." Perhaps the sincerity of that vision and the surrounding cultural apparatus that sustained it are some of the reasons why we now imbue Formica laminate with just a touch of nostalgia for those years.

Simon Leong

Notes

1   Perry M. Lamek, "Brooks Stevens: Designing the American Dream," *Milwaukee* (August 1987), 48.

2   Ibid., 128.

3   From a speech given by Stevens, "Industrial Designer's Approach to Passenger Car Styling," which appeared in *Canadian Railway Club* 43 (November 13, 1950), 28.

4   Stevens, Brooks. Telephone interview with author, December 1989.

5   Industrial Designer's Approach, 29.

4 | 22

97

4 23

FORMICA
AND DINERS

The classic diner was a building that called attention to itself by its use of materials. This was always true on the exterior: The shape of the building was unique, and it was covered with sleek stainless steel and bright porcelain enamel, all set off with glowing neon. It was also the case inside where a colorful, flashy environment was crafted of stainless steel, ceramic tile, chrome, glass, mirrors, marble, and laminate.

Diners were industrial buildings constructed in factories. The diner manufacturers always made use of new materials and "products of the future" as soon as they were available. One does well to remember that the traditional diner was a vernacular building designed and assembled by craftsmen—carpenters, metal workers, tile setters—not by architects or other professional designers. The images they turned to for inspiration came from the railroad, the airplane, and other icons of the machine age.

The interior of the diner was a machine for the cooking and serving of food in an expedient manner. The basic layout was fixed early on: a long counter with stools running the length of the diner, with food preparation taking place behind. Thereafter, only the diner's size and its look were altered to keep pace with the demands of customers and the latest style. All the working parts of the kitchen—and the cook—were in plain view behind the counter, offset by shimmering stainless steel

4-23
Formica laminate-topped tables designed by Edward Wormley in the 1950s. As a surfacing material, Formica laminate found its application on furniture which was both innovative and whimsical. *Photos courtesy of Parsons School of Design.*

4-24
John C. Roeser, Jr. and Hattie Roeser, proprieters of the oldest family owned bakery in Chicago (founded in 1911), in their newly remodeled shop. The installation used Frost Walnut Picwood Formica laminate on all paneling, pie fronts, and cornices. *Photo courtesy of John C. Roeser, III.*

4-25
A model home kitchen of the late 1950s featuring Formica laminate.

appliances and cabinets tended to be freestanding, 1950s' kitchens were notable for their sleek, unified look. Kitchens were sometimes described as "scientific" and, certainly in appearance, were transformed into Mom's "laboratory," full of smooth, sparkling surfaces.

Industry retooled after the war: New dies were created for appliances, and new uses were found for materials that had gone into the war effort. Manufacturers like Republic Steel began fabricating complete modular layouts that needed only the addition of plastic laminated surfaces and appliances to create a finished kitchen. Laminate was what pulled the design together, in the form of counter tops, backsplashes, and "island" work areas.

in sunburst patterns.

The diner builders achieved an overall harmonious look with hard surfaces that were easy to keep shiny and clean, prerequisites for the food-service business. When Formica decorative laminates became available in the 1930s, they were immediately put to use in diner interiors. At first, Formica laminate panels were used in ceilings, replacing wood or metal sheeting. A cigarette-burn proof grade was developed for counter tops and tabletops, and this began to replace the traditional marble, wood, or glass.

The hard edges and sheer surfaces of Formica laminate fit in perfectly with the diner aesthetic, which glorified the beauty of the machine. With the seventy colors available in 1940, and inlays of one color over another, the decorative possibilities

As the center of the home, the kitchen became the place where families enjoyed many of their meals, and the built-in or freestanding dining table became the heart of the room. Another kitchen innovation was the "dinette," a furniture item that reached its glory days in the 1950s. It consisted of a chrome frame combined with a brightly colored laminate top, the result being a convenient, low-maintenance dining area. With storage drawers beneath the tabletop and its smooth surface, the table could double as a work area outside of mealtimes.

Similar developments were taking place in the bathroom, with the Formica Company itself promoting one of the central ideas. Formica advertising of the era

4-26
Neff's Diner,
Allentown, PA.
Photo courtesy of
R. J. S. Gutman.

4-27
This colorful restaurant from the 1950s called on bright new colors from The Sunrise Color Line and an inlaid bar and tabletops to create a fanciful ocean theme in Formica laminate.

were virtually endless, and this was very appealing to diner owners and builders. There were standard inlaid patterns available in different color schemes for tabletops, usually incorporating stripes, circles, or other geometric shapes. One custom design featured an inlaid graphic of a steaming coffee cup. Decorative inlaid panels with Art Deco graphics above the windows and on the range hood were popular during the World War II era.

In the postwar period, with a few exceptions, laminate became the only material used for counter tops in diners. By the end of the decade, laminate also covered interior doors and some of the wall surfaces previously faced with tile. This coincided with the postwar building boom in the suburbs, where Formica laminate reigned supreme in home kitchens as well. Many

of the new suburban homes included a dinette, where a built-in booth featured a laminate tabletop. The diner's "home away from home" atmosphere was thus mirrored by the transposing of its elements into residential use.

The availability of Formica laminate in marbleized and wood-grain patterns helped usher in a big change in the diner look in the late 1950s. Feeling pressure from the burgeoning fast-food industry, diner owners shifted gears and expanded the size of their menus and buildings. The wood-grain laminates provided a new surburban image. With the addition of a few wagon-wheel light fixtures, and some coach lamps and bay windows on the exterior, the colonial diner was born. As Americana took hold, fake beams were clad in wood-grain Formica laminate, and the diner took

often features the "Vanitory," a built-in cabinet under the lavatory, heralded as an essential new bathroom fixture. This idea was hailed as practical and beautiful and was promoted as an area where Mom could apply makeup and generally pamper herself. In the bathroom, too, plastic laminates were used as a replacement for ceramic tiles on wall surfaces.

Many manufacturers created laminate furniture for other rooms of the house, particularly the living room, where it could take a lot of punishment from children and pets. Normally used in its wood-grained variations here, Formica laminate found its most popular furniture application in tables, which sometimes featured slim, wrought-iron legs. This application did not seem to *on a rec-room appearance.*

The diner renaissance that began in the 1980s has been characterized by a longing for the old, familiar railroad-style diner. Furthermore, it has brought about a renewed interest in some of the old Formica laminate patterns, once standard but now either discontinued or hard to get. The Linen pattern, in charcoal, primrose, green, gray, powder blue, tan, pink, and lipstick red, was to be found in nearly every diner of the forties and early fifties. Now it is available by special order only. The Boomerang pattern was also a big hit when it was introduced in the early fifties. It is now back by popular demand (it was reintroduced in 1988) in charcoal, white, light blue, and pink.

People have been living with Formica laminate in their kitchens for the past forty years. They have grown accustomed to it— its versatility, its color. The diner is the kitchen of America, and Formica laminate has been an important part of it.

Richard J. S. Gutman

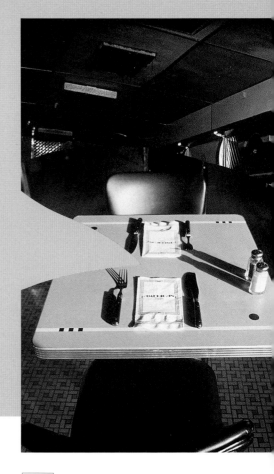

take hold in the same way that plastic laminates did in the kitchen, however, and in subsequent decades manufacturers have returned to wood furniture for the living room, and have experimented with materials like glass, chrome, and molded plastic.

Outside the home, Formica laminate became the most popular surface material for soda-fountain counters, airplane interiors, retail cabinets, and many other commercial furnishings. Its variety of colors and patterns presented designers with endless possibilities, and it was a practical and inexpensive alternative to wood. Today, it is difficult to imagine how commercial interiors were constructed *without* the material.

Although Formica laminate had been around for decades, it was this postwar era that made it indispensable. Versatile, inexpensive, and easy to fabricate, it was a willing partner in the postwar building boom. Simply stated, it was in the right place at the right time.

4-28
Willow Grove Diner,
Willow Grove, PA.
Photo: R. J. S. Gutman.

4-29
American Diner,
Princeton, NJ.
Photo: R. J. S. Gutman.

4-30
This 1950s advertisement equates Formica laminate tabletops with good restaurant management.

HIT PARADE OF DINERS

Mickey's Dining Car, St. Paul, MN, 1937
Walls, ceiling, and counter tops covered with Formica laminate.

Edgemere Diner, Shrewsbury, MA, late 1940s
Inlaid tabletops and decorative panels in pink and rose.

Bel-Aire Diner, West Peabody, MA, 1950s
Pink, pearl, and gray Linen and Boomerang Formica laminate patterns.

Elgin Diner, Camden, NJ, 1959
Marbleized counter and tabletops, driftwood-grain wall and door coverings.

Silver Diner, Rockville, MD, 1989
Two-tone ceiling in pink Boomerang and tan Linen.

4 | 28

...tyle IN FORMICA TABLE TOPS

4 | 30

105

Notes

1 Joseph C. Goulden, *The Best Years: 1945–50* (New York: Atheneum, 1976), 135–37.

2 Betty Friedan, *The Feminine Mystique* (New York: W. W. Norton & Company, Inc., 1963), 246.

3 Thomas Hine, *Populuxe* (New York: Alfred A. Knopf, Inc., 1986), 3–14.

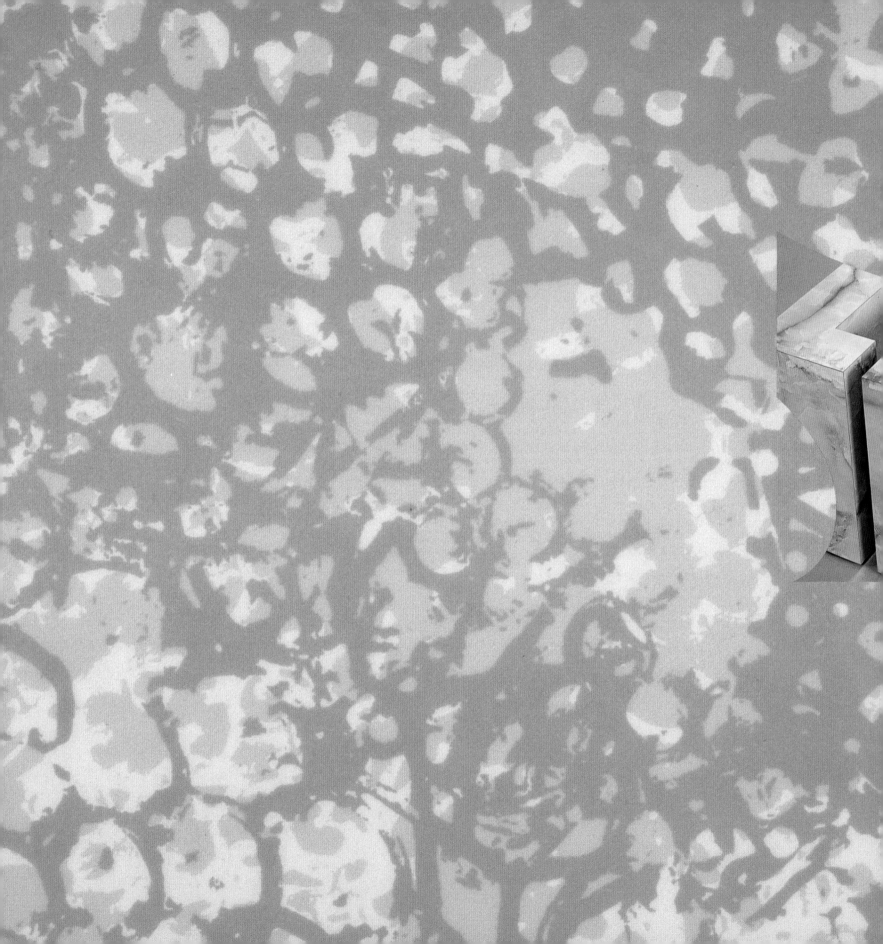

Sarah Bodine and Michael Dunas

Plastic Expression

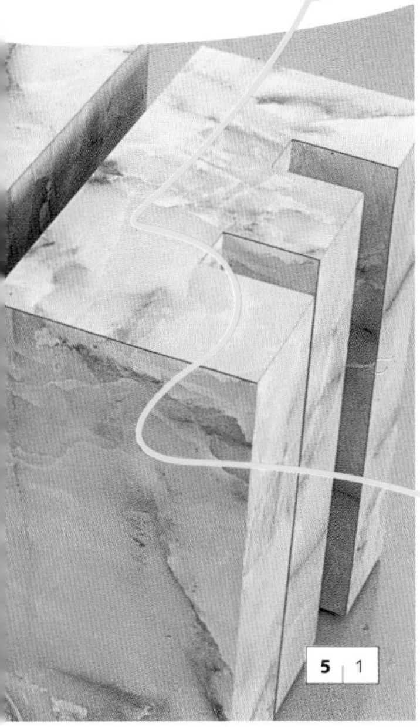

5 | 1

Chapter **5**

The essential fact of any artwork is the material it is made of, what we might consider the concrete aspect of its meaning. Seeing, touching, smelling the object induce immediate visceral reactions, which, in almost the same instant trigger remembrances of a variety of occasions when the same material was influential. Proust's mnemonic encounter with the madeleine might find a present-day equivalent in an encounter with chrome, fiber glass, or polyurethane.

As we accrue associations with a material we become increasingly familiar with its physical properties and the circumstances of its use. Too often, however, in this heyday of science and technology, mining a material experience isn't that easy. The secure knowledge of metal, wood, paint, glass, and so on—the foundations of the material world of yesterday—once required of the consumer pales in comparison to what is expected of us in a modern synthetic environment. In finding ourselves living with Naugahyde sleepers, rhinestone cowboys, and Teflon presidents, do we fully appreciate their material implications? Are

5-1
Nancy Dwyer, <u>Lie,</u> 1986.
*Photo courtesy of
Josh Baer Gallery.*

5-2
Tom Loeser, <u>Chest of
Drawers</u>, 1985.
*Photo courtesy of
Tom Loeser.*

5-3
Jack A. Willard,
<u>Cornucopia</u>, 1955.
*Photo courtesy of
Mrs. Jack A. Willard.*

109

we mindful of how our view of the world has changed each time there has been an inventive shift in its chemistry?

The whole family of plastic laminates, including Formica brand laminate and ColorCore surfacing material, has in its short history already garnered a distinctive reputation as a modern material. Relatively inexpensive, laminates are egalitarian, displayed proudly in households of every social class. Durable and virtually maintenance-free, they are symbols of a clean, well-kept place. As synthetics, they testify to a civilizing ingenuity, and as "plastics," they offer a future of unlimited options. By extension, then, they might well represent current domestic values.

For Richard Artschwager, who is credited as the first major American artist to take Formica laminate as his primary medium, there is apparently even more to plastic laminate's image. In the sixties, when laminate was moving out of the kitchen and into boutiques, Artschwager was cladding sculptures that resembled furniture with sheets of wood-grain laminate—the most blatantly ersatz of all the Formica laminate patterns. With deadpan humor, he saw the potential for creating painterly illusion with recognizable three-dimensional objects, namely chairs and tables. Laminate, that great, ugly material of our age, was the perfect representation of wood; it conveyed the right image without authentic properties like tactility, depth of grain, and color. The patterned material transformed the furniture into an image of compressed abstraction, reflecting ambient light and infinite space. Confronting the viewer with what can be described as a perplexed stare, laminate pushed the image of furniture into two dimensions, thereby jogging our way of seeing without challenging our knowledge of materials and construction techniques.

What distinguishes Artschwager's work is his realization that laminate embodies its own contradiction, that there is no need for additional explanation of or justification for the material's metaphoric usage in an artwork. Our seeing laminate as *faux* allows it to remain an everyday material and at the same time to become the subject for something else, in Artschwager's case, real wood. In this age of simulation, Artschwager has circumvented the thorny dilemma of the authenticity of the creative act by pointing to the irony of laminate, letting this original *faux* material become a truth that bears the burden of slippery identities. Artschwager accepts laminate as a postmodern material, with all the problems and efficacies afforded by a current contextual reading. He goes about his business of constructing furniture-inspired sculpture, leaving the problems of what is to become of the piece and the role material plays to the viewer, whose obligation it is to piece together the relevant bits of information that constitute materials communication in a materialist world.

Like Artschwager, conceptual artist Douglas Huebler used solid Formica laminate sheets as a surface material over plywood in the mid-1960s. Huebler's minimal sculptures resemble large-scale Chinese puzzle pieces or children's blocks. Their exaggerated sawtooth edges, chiseled S-curves, and jagged asymmetrical ledges would seem to interlock, if joined, to form a giant tetrahedron. In this work, Formica laminate provided the prerequisite sanitized surface of a toy, while the suggestion of an overscaled plaything helped humanize the anonymous character of the material.

As an artist who came into prominence in the 1980s, Nancy Dwyer has contrived to upend the literal meanings of public and private, mind and body, high art and popular culture, through the irony of Formica laminate. Using words as images, constructed in large scale with Formica laminate sheet, she finds ways to change our relationship to the world not only as we see or feel it but also as we read it. What is obviously accessible in Dwyer's work—the simple words and rudimentary constructions—has an uncanny ability to dislodge obvious meanings in its presentation. The directness and simplicity of Formica laminate, complementing the word/image, compels us to go beyond the superficial. The sign, a material word/image, raises profound questions: Do we say what we mean? Do we know what we see? We are drawn into these ruminations by the realization that language is as much a determinant of reality as is physical nature. When familiar words such as *lie* or *lazy* are clothed in laminate, they become the language of a new representation, paradoxically magnified by a material that disguises their physical properties.

Given time, however, these objects are engaging—physically, viscerally, almost erotically. Although Dwyer is attempting to communicate quickly with her audience, there is still something deeply hidden in her work, forcing the viewer to encounter that which cannot be literally described. Passivity is not possible in the presence of cold communication. Most of Dwyer's sculptures are unequivocally personal, domestic even, though she uses strategies of advertising and memorialization more appropriate to the public arena. In the end, what Dwyer wants is an engagement, a "negotiation," that requires the viewer to construct the work's meaning, with little help from the artist. This active reception on the viewer's part turns recognition into a creative act.

In the 1960s, when Formica laminate was coerced into use as a cladding material for sculpture that commented on familiar objects like furniture and toys, artists like Billy Al Bengston were also commandeering it as a canvas on which to paint. In a series from 1965, with titles like "Tubesteak," "Meatball," and "Guayuli Kid," Bengston used wood-grain and pseudotextured counter-top Formica laminate in roughly kitchen-table-sized (2-by-3-foot) sheets as backdrops on which to stencil and airbrush a combination of military and occult imagery. If Artschwager was working with the three-dimensional illusion of Formica laminate, Bengston was adamant about its flatness. This was in keeping with the aesthetic of pop art, which sought to render graphically, in a machinelike, anonymous way, without expression or gesture, the enigmas of popular culture: How close to its source can a work of art be and still preserve its identity? How many kinds of signs can a work of art be at once? All of the signs used by Bengston—the surface of the Formica laminate, the military insignia, and the occult radiant eye—were clearly either part of the establishment or part of the counterculture during the sixties. By superimposing these diverse signs on Formica laminate, Bengston challenged the "psychic" as well as the real distance between these beliefs.

While laminate's subtext as an art material that relates to popular culture has remained constant, the means by which it has been manipulated have become increasingly sophisticated in the eighties. Rather than using the Formica product in sheet form, French artist Jean-Lucien Guillaume has shredded the laminate to develop a "stratified straw" material (*paille stratifiée*), which is then made into paneling and used to re-cover or wrap the pedestals

of public sculptures and the façades of buildings, as well as being made into self-supporting wall mounts. Guillaume's intention is not to hide the sculpture's original granite, marble, or stone, nor to redecorate it, but to see it as a construction material of the mind, refitting the common forms and objects of everyday life in order to draw attention once more to the structures, to redefine their forms as textural planes in the streetscape. Another series, "Modul'Art," explores the use of shredded Formica laminate as a painterly medium to produce graphic images, such as road maps, musical scores, and street graphics. These textural patterns, sinuous and spaghettilike, are both ready-made, found objects, seemingly anonymously mounted for display, and a commentary about the 1980s' obsession with refitting the earth with industrially produced products.

Working with Formica laminate in Barcelona, John Richardson is one of the few painters to use the material as a canvas. The smooth, nonporous surface led him to achieve consistent and permanent strokes, brilliancy of color, and a clear delineation between background and foreground through the use of another product of modern technology—magic markers. The combination of these two new art materials, however, did not lead Richardson to produce works of a space-age slickness; instead, his imagery is primitive, almost childlike, the brightly painted faces, energized line, and obsessive handwriting forming a rhythmic patterning. Richardson has created a primal hieroglyph using new-age materials, affirming that the artist remains human and innocent, even when working with the most advanced materials science can provide.

5 | 4

5-4
Richard Artschwager,
Chair Table, 1980.
Photo courtesy of
Leo Castelli.

5-5
Richard Artschwager,
Blue Logus, 1967.
Photo courtesy of
Leo Castelli.

113

Equally primitive in inspiration but more slick in execution are the pieces by Dan Friedman made for his special African theme show at Art et Industrie gallery in New York in 1986. In fashioning Formica laminate plywood, straw, and metal into both blatant and subtle images, Friedman attempted to show the erratic shift in the content of life in native and amalgamated cultures in today's world. Friedman treated Formica laminate over plywood as found refuse of an industrial culture, which he used to form decorative objects—such as bright red, black, yellow, and green end tables in the outline of the African continent—much as a rural African might treat spark plugs as belt danglers or use tin cans to make briefcases and boxes. Art becomes the mediator between the two cultures, expressing how the "sophisticated" can seem to be "primitive" and how the so-called primitive is actually highly sophisticated.

Ostensibly, Russell Forester also exploits the color potential of Formica laminate in his laminate-clay-plywood constructions that resemble three-dimensional backlit renditions of Suprematist paintings. The difference is, of course, the technology—not paint but plastic laminate for color, and not external spotlights but internal miniature neon bulbs and LEDs to illuminate the planar structures. These are the space-age electronic toys of the eighties, which look like extraterrestrial beings, yet which house, on close inspection, a playful combination of miniature country and suburban tableaux. At first glance, Forester's work is pleasing and novel, yet it subtly plays on the ways in which synthetics have changed the way we perceive the world, and more importantly,

5-6
Nancy Dwyer, EZ, 1987.
Photo courtesy of Josh Baer Gallery.

5-7
Nancy Dwyer, Lie, 1986.
Photo courtesy of Josh Baer Gallery.

5-8
Douglas Huebler, Truro Series #1, 1966.
Photo courtesy of Douglas Huebler.

5-9
Jean-Lucien Guillaume, Untitled, 1985.

5 | 6

5 | 7

5 | 8

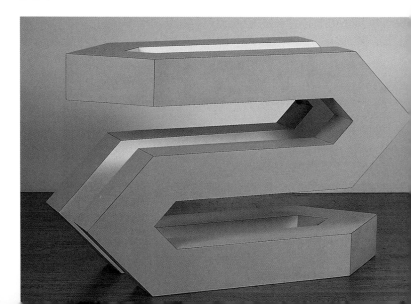

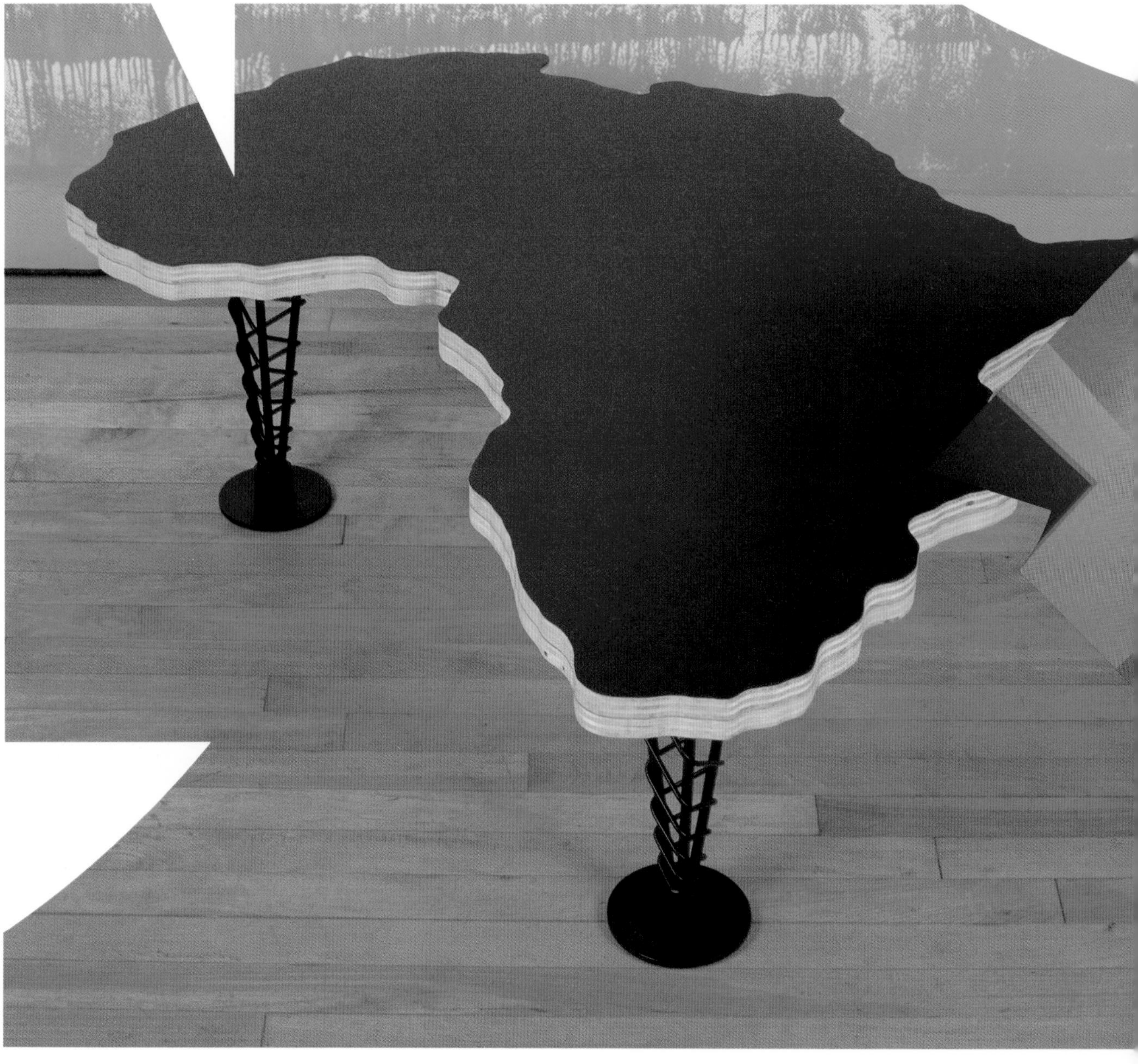

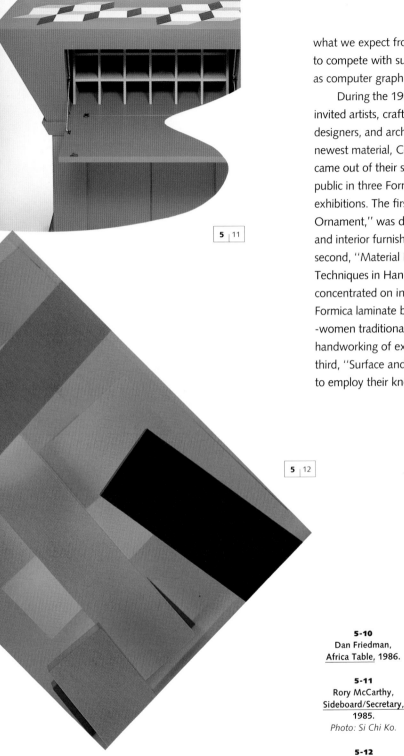

what we expect from an artwork as it tries to compete with such perceptual dynamics as computer graphics.

During the 1980s Formica Corporation invited artists, craftsmen and -women, designers, and architects to explore its newest material, ColorCore. The work that came out of their studios was first made public in three Formica-sponsored traveling exhibitions. The first, "Surface & Ornament," was devoted to architectural and interior furnishings by designers; the second, "Material Evidence: New Color Techniques in Handmade Furniture," concentrated on innovative applications of Formica laminate by craftsmen and -women traditionally trained in the fine handworking of exotic woods; and the third, "Surface and Edge," invited jewelers to employ their knowledge of precious

5-10
Dan Friedman,
Africa Table, 1986.

5-11
Rory McCarthy,
Sideboard/Secretary,
1985.
Photo: Si Chi Ko.

5-12
Russel Forrester,
Untitled, 1985.

metals and gemstones in working ColorCore as a decorative element of obdurate beauty in its own right.

Plastic laminate is not foreign to architects or craftsmen and -women and is certainly not an innovation of the eighties, but its increasing importance as an art material with expressive potential for design became evident in these three shows. With the introduction of ColorCore, not only did designers have an ersatz material with synthetic qualities like plastic, but also a laminate that could be worked "honestly," like a natural material. ColorCore's elimination of the black edge, which previously had detracted from the volumetric potential of the sheet, made it appear to be a densely colored solid with a strong palpable mass. The stability and consistency of the material in sheet form rendered it workable with the methods traditionally employed on wood, metal, and stone. It could be sawed, routed, etched, sandblasted, or scored, the only restriction being that since it was heat-formed, the laminate, for most uses, had to be cold-connected—glued, riveted, punctured, or linked. ColorCore's honesty in fabrication also allowed designers to appreciate the material's properties through an expression of technology and structure. The material could now take its place among other constructive materials as an essential part of the design concept, not mere decorative excess but a prime component of the composition.

While artists such as Scott Burton and Neil Jenny used Formica laminate in their furniture in the late seventies, handcraftsmen and -women had been skeptical of using such synthetic material in serious furniture pieces. The "Material

117

Evidence'' exhibition saw furniture makers take the leap from an attitude toward furniture as an expression of material and function to furniture as a psychological connection between form and meaning. The introduction of the ''honest'' laminate ColorCore freed new American furniture makers to experiment with the implications of an expanding range of rhetorical possibilities. This experimentation manifested itself in a number of different optical effects, including complex new-wave patterning and illusionistic, trompe l'oeil, and *faux* effects, to establish a contemporary language of decoration.

Patterning on furniture took on a whole new dimension with the introduction of ColorCore. While the material was new, however, the techniques employed in working it were those of traditional woodworking: inlay, beveling, and carving. Tom Loeser used mosaic in his triangulated ''Chest of Drawers,'' in which randomly placed squares of strong and subtle colors in ColorCore and paint animate the surfaces of the suspended drawers. This piece combines the conceptual play on the function of a chest of drawers as a sort of interrupted teepee with the visual activity of an op art painting. Multiple ColorCore chips keep the eye racing up and down the frontal plane of the chest, with the diminishing size of the cantilevered drawers adding to the perceptual energy. Knowing that portability has been a hallmark of Loeser's furniture leads us to conclude that he would like us to reformulate our feelings about chests, to realize that they can be makeshift-looking yet sturdy, airy rather than massive, and visually stimulating rather than ponderously prosaic.

5-13
Billy Al Bengston,
Tubesteak, 1965.
Photo courtesy of
Billy Al Bengston.

5-14
John Richardson,
La Noche, 1981.
Photo courtesy of
Georges Richardson.

A different kind of illusion is created in Rory McCarthy's "Sideboard/Secretary," in which the choice of a Burnt Sienna ColorCore matte sheet gives the initial impression of a warm wood. This feeling is reinforced by the simulation of volumetric blocks on the top, which, although flat, play off actual cubbyholes inside the desk compartment. This piece metaphorically addresses the ongoing dilemma between applied and fine art, that is, which reality is more functional—the practical necessity of a place to put things or the ephemeral stimulation of the illusion of floating volume?

Complex patterning and illusionism are also apparent in Tom Lacagnina's "Octagon Table," in which small wedges of multilayered ColorCore "sandwiches" at each corner encourage the belief that the density of the top pattern exists throughout the depth of the tabletop. The small octagonal lens set in the middle of the tabletop is reminiscent of a giant

5 | 14

kaleidoscope, through which one might be able to see the multiple permutations of pattern and color that must exist beneath the tabletop. This piece comments on the inner life of furniture—and, by extension, the thought process behind furniture—which predetermines the outcome of the surface but is never seen after the piece is completed.

Architectural rustication and *faux* effects are employed by Rick Wrigley in his "Armoire," a furniture-sized rendition of a classical portico. Here, through scoring, tearing, and layering, the versatile ColorCore laminate is used to imitate stone, plasterwork, and masonry. Wrigley's exercise provides a twist on the commonly held notion that lamination of any kind is a falsification of the construction material. Here the eroding of the rustification does not expose real brickwork (or even the plywood that forms the structure of the "Armoire"); rather, it reveals another incarnation of ColorCore and seems to be playing with the idea of "honest" materials and the property of ColorCore all the way through.

Almost since its invention in the United States in 1868, plastic has been used in jewelry. As an inexpensive substitute for ivory, tortoiseshell, and amber, it was prevalent in Victorian jewelry, and during the ebullient twenties, brightly colored Bakelite satisfied consumers' desires for theatrical, ephemeral, and garish costume jewelry. Most recently, the 1981 exhibition "Good as Gold: Alternative Materials in American Jewelry," sponsored by the Smithsonian Institution Traveling Exhibition Service, surveyed the full range of possibilities of using plastic in contemporary jewelry. The expansive use of cast polyester

5 | 15

5 | 18

resin, Ceconite, acrylic tubing, Lucite, and vinyl confirmed the dominant role of synthetics as viable alternatives to precious gold and silver.

In contrast, the "Surface and Edge" exhibition, sponsored by Formica Corporation, did not aim to continue the exploitation of plastic as a substitute for the real thing, as a cheap imitation of fine jewelry. The challenge of "Surface and Edge" was for ColorCore to be accepted as a new "gem" of the modern age. For jewelers, this meant that the traditional values of color and structure possessed by gold, silver, and precious stones had to be seen as intrinsic to the plastic sheet and discrete. They could not rely on ColorCore as merely an extraneous enrichment or symbolic detachment but rather had to view it as the essential element at the heart of wearable pride and dignity.

121

5-15
Ivy Ross/Robert Ebendorf, ColorCore necklace, 1986.

5-16
Hiroko Sato and Gene Pijanowski, head ornament, 1986.

5-17
Thomas Gentille, Légion d'Honneur, armlet, 1987.

5-18
Pavel Opočenský, Surell brooches, 1990.
Photos: Jan Frank Photography.

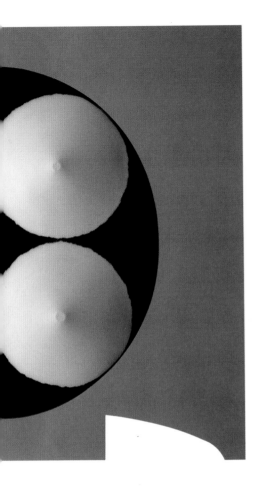

5-19
Pavel Opočenský,
ColorCore brooches,
1988.
*Photos: Jan Frank
Photography.*

This structural quality is perhaps the single most important contribution made by the new ColorCore laminate to jewelry. It is possible now to think of color as the structural core of the piece, as it has been for centuries with gold and gemstones.

Bob Ebendorf and Ivy Ross approached the problem of bead making with the new laminate. Through irregular cutting and layering, they were able to fabricate intricate and changeable beads that simulated traditional glass-bead-patterning, millefiori effects, achieved through the controlled positioning of positive and negative spaces on the circumference of the plastic bead. From a distance, the colorful banding on the surface of these geometric beads seems continuous, while on close inspection it becomes clear that their cores are eaten away and distorted in asymmetrical progressions to provide an illusionistic, translucent effect.

The potential for opaque color has also encouraged exploration of the use of ColorCore graphically. This is evident in pieces by a number of jewelers in the "Surface and Edge" exhibition, including Rebekah Laskin, Suzanne Bucher, Alice Klein, and Vernon Reed. The thinness of the laminate sheet allows the overlapping of multiple-shaped pieces which are cut out, punched, etched, and riveted together, while still keeping the depth of the piece to a jewelry scale. This flat, two-dimensional approach allows ColorCore to act as an animating element, almost cartoonlike in its whimsical shapes, bright hues, and dynamic compositions. In the case of these jewelers, ColorCore has become a substitute for opaque enamels, colored reactive metals, or anodized aluminum, all of which have recently been mustered to emphasize the

123

1980's nonprecious attitude toward the making, collecting, and wearing of jewelry.

The small scale of jewelry has traditionally encouraged a virtuoso treatment of materials. The response elicited from a material is the basis for a series of "Head Ornaments" made in ColorCore and plastic by Hiroko Sato and Gene Pijanowski. While this work is ostensibly based on traditional Japanese helmet and ritual headgear design, it is the correspondence of the fabrication materials that makes a statement. The properties of ColorCore, opacity and structural strength, even the process by which it is made, are surprisingly similar to those of the special paper originally used in traditional helmets. This paper, made from the bark of the paper mulberry tree, was pasted in many layers and laminated to a linen cloth in order to create a form for the helmet. ColorCore also corresponds to the lacquered wood of the helmets in its ability to add color to the flamboyant shapes. The use of ColorCore in these helmets represents an assertion that the spectacular effect of plastic laminate is as appropriate to the modern sensibility as traditional natural materials—paper, leather, and lacquered wood—were in the past.

A subtle interface of color and surface is achieved by Pavel Opočenský in his sensual, organic brooches made from a special lamination of white and black ColorCore. Opočenský employs the carving techniques he previously used to manipulate ivory and ebony to depress and erode the white surface layers, revealing a sometimes translucent, sometimes hard edge surrounding the black underlayer, and to create an ethereal surface silhouette. In this way he disproves a commonly held

belief that "natural" materials, that is, those produced by nature, are uniquely able to reveal an inner substance of beauty. Chiaroscuro effects on the starkly elemental shapes of Opočenský's brooches evoke a respect for the inherent power of this synthetic material to elicit intimacy.

That search for material essence has been achieved with ColorCore by Thomas Gentille in his series of circular armlets, which, along with his other works, were shown at the Victoria and Albert Museum

5 | 21

5 | 20

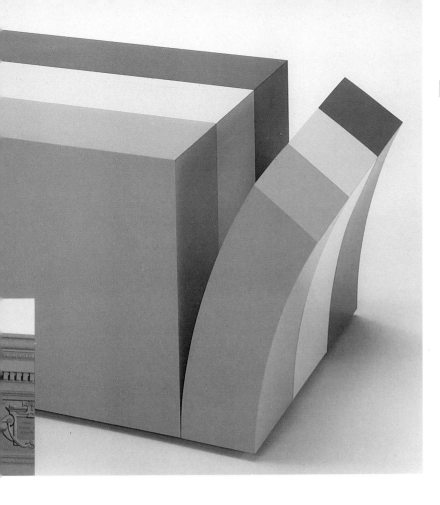

5 | 22

5-20
Tom Lacagnina,
<u>Octagon Table,</u> 1985.
*Photo courtesy of
American Craft Council,
© 1985.*

5-21
Rick Wrigley,
<u>Armoire,</u> 1985.
Photo: Si Chi Ko.

5-22
Lee Payne,
<u>Neapolitan,</u> 1983.
*Photo: Hedrich-Blessing,
Chicago.*

in 1987. Rather than exploring the correspondence of ColorCore to other materials, however, Gentille looks to its intrinsic properties, to ColorCore for its own sake, as have a number of Modernist painters searching for the essence of visual perception with purest color. Thus, his tour-de-force armlet, "Légion d'Honneur," reveals the subtle perceptual relationship of the material through the simple layering of white on white. This piece uses light, shadows, and reflections, the clear articulation of the crisp, stepped layers, to speak of the infinite quality of the material.

In their use of laminate, and particularly ColorCore, artists and craftsmen and -women have succeeded in mining a familiar material in new ways—a material that can be used to mirror our lives as well as to change them. The challenge of such versatility rivals the introduction of acrylics in painting or synthetic materials in weaving. The aggressive use of ColorCore by artists and craftsmen and -women has stimulated a new perception of material value, a reexamination of what material honesty means, and a heightened recognition of the inventive shifts in the chemistry of the world today.

6 | 1

6 | 2

Sarah Bayliss

THE LAMINATE WOMAN: FORMICA IN WOMEN'S LIVES

Chapter **6**

127

Simon Leung

WOOD GRAINS

137

It is no secret that historians of American home design have compared the care of the home with the care of the female body. From the nineteenth century on, two related themes guided much design theory: the home as a metaphor for a woman's body, and the belief that "femininity" in the home would enhance the womanhood of its

mistress, creating a wholesome domestic atmosphere. It was assumed that thoughtful wives and mothers would create a genteel household climate reflecting their own characters. An 1861 article entitled "The Final Cause of Woman" advised that "the more womanly a woman is, the more likely she is to throw her personality over the home, and transform it into a sort of outermost garment of her soul."[1] Investing household objects with femininity confirmed not only that a feminine look was desirable but that femininity could be

6-1
Formica Girl
(detail), 1960s.

6-2
This happy homemaker
turned happy fabricator
demonstrates the ease
and versatility of
Flakeboard, a Formica
brand product in use
during the 1960s.

6-3
A 1960s woman with her
Formica furniture—at
ease, at home.
Both are elegant, highly
styled, with equally
lacquered surfaces.

6-4
In this promotional
image from the early
1960s, a young woman's
face is compared
to Formica
sample chips.

6-5
A woman with her
waterproof "Formica
garden" in a 1970 ad.
The pseudonatural pin-
up look confirms a
departure from maternal
personas like
"Mrs. America."

invented, or bought, in the form of furniture and household goods. New appliances and chemicals that emerged in the late nineteenth century perplexed the home-woman metaphor by inspiring a scientific approach to household care. As housecleaning came to be perceived as a more technological undertaking, the concerns of feminine values and a scientific attitude intersected as primary issues in home decoration. These associations would eventually influence the feminization of commodities in twentieth-century advertising.

Formica brand laminate reemphasized these associations when it entered millions of American homes during the 1940s and 1950s. In terms of style, laminate transformed the traditional "woman's space" of the kitchen into the most streamlined, modern room in the house. It enabled women to custom-design working spaces to their exact liking, renewing a sense of pride in the housewife "lifestyle." And by combining the latest scientific and stylistic advances in home design, Formica laminate strengthened consumer associations between technology and femininity. Advertisements likened the surface of Formica laminate to women's skin, and Formica laminate's colors and patterns evolved to suit prevailing fashion. Laminate's total efficiency enhanced the idea of a scientifically oriented housewife. The ideological image would reach its height after World War II as a picture of femininity that was spartan, home-oriented, and efficient.

But while Formica laminate glamorized women's place in the kitchen, it also helped fulfill the notion that women belonged in the house rather than elsewhere. A 1955

6-6
A woman in the kitchen, ca. 1900.

6-7
A kitchen built in 1920 shows a gas stove, but built-in counters and dinettes had not appeared yet.

6-8
Formica Corporation's kitchen for the 1964 World's Fair House. The company proposed a "carefree" house with "exciting wipe clean materials on walls, doors, cabinets, counters and even furniture." One-hundred and sixty-seven regional variations of this "House of the Future" were built in the United States.

6-9
Toward the early 1960s, the Formica laminate kitchen at times became an elaborate site for fantasy. It was during this time that the "open-plan" kitchen appeared everywhere in suburban American homes, a design devised to allow Mom to survey the house from her "centrally located station."

6-10
This ColorCore kitchen designed by Peter Shire is both fun and functional. His imaginative use of ColorCore surfacing material creates a continuous and colorful pattern without the interference associated with the black line of traditional laminate.

6-11
This Formica wood-grain laminate kitchen from the late 1960s represents the ultimate cooking command post for Mom. Her preparation space is doubled with the addition of a second free-floating island.

6 | 6

6 | 9

6 | 10

6 | 7

6 | 8

6 | 11

Formica advertisement shows a housewife mulling over her choices of counter colors. She advises her readers, "Some colors bring out the best features in a gal and others do less than nothing for her." She chooses the color of Formica laminate most flattering to her complexion, and, it would follow, looks forward to years of beauty in the kitchen.

Product advertising had been sharpening its pitch to women for many years when the laminate boom hit. A scientific approach to housecleaning had been developing (and becoming increasingly sophisticated) since 1914, the year electrical appliances first came into the home. Advertising encouraged women to take a scientific approach to housework, glorifying an antiseptic look and lifestyle. While the images often carried woman-to-woman tips about wise consumerism, the texts tended to dictate new, impeccable standards for household and personal beauty. One advertisement from 1929 pictured a Hollywood starlet recommending household cleaning fluid with the advice, "Beauty must be spotless," comparing the appeal of a germ-free house with the allure of a woman's spotless complexion.

Depression-era media catalyzed an antiseptic craze in other ways. Promoters played on consumer paranoia by associating disease with an unclean kitchen. Everywhere, women in magazines delivered warnings to other women about pollutants festering in every eave and grout line. In 1927 an advertisement for electricity advised, "For health's sake, use electricity." And a lengthy 1918 ad for Lysol disinfectant asked, "Is your home germ-haunted? The germ-haunted house shelters a menace that is far from imaginary, which is dangerously

6-12
The objective of "subtle leg beauty" was "a flattering male glance" according to this advertisement for nylon hosiery which appeared in the early 1950s.

6-13
Formica laminates in patterns, wood grains, and solid colors are incorporated in this high-style 1960s kitchen.

6-14
This decorative, multi-functional 1960s room functions as a laundry room, linen closet, and luxurious wash room complete with velvet ottoman.

real. Science has shown a way to eradicate these dangers. . . . " Because the housewife was allegedly empowered to protect her family from these evils, women's place in the home seemed critical. Formica laminate's potential for total spotlessness suited those who believed in the pacifying effect of hyper-cleanliness in the home as well as in the wife. In the postwar American mind-set, the neat housewife symbolized economic and moral normality, as pursuing the antiseptic became a standard household concern.

Most products featured in women's magazines such as *Woman's Day* during the 1940s and 1950s continued to stress the housewife's responsibility for family hygiene and food preparation. In 1945 one advertising strategist urged salesmen to help the housewife "justify her menial task by building up her role as protector of the family—the killer of millions of microbes and germs. . . . Make housework a matter of knowledge and skill, rather than a matter of brawn and dull, un-remitting effort."[2] New products such as instant food and plastic wrap were part of the "easy," antiseptic life of which Formica laminate was iconic. But the message of liberation from kitchen drudgery promised by these images belied the fact that such attention to hygiene was obsessive, costly, and unnecessary. (It was also very time-consuming, so in a sense one replaced drudgery with drudgery of another sort.) One television ad for plastic wrap depicted "Mom" preparing for a picnic by wrapping food, silverware, baby shoes, and her husband's baseball cap in plastic film, only to unwrap it all later at a roadside picnic table.

For many young women after World War II, "home" was a place of mixed

133

messages. There was the wife's empowerment as germ killer in a custom-designed kitchen, but also her economic dependence on her husband. The ad-world homemakers appearing in Formica or copycat Formica laminate kitchens often served as role models for housewives seeking glamor in their own lives. Many wives who had given up their wartime jobs to returning veterans experienced emotional conflict: Despite the plentiful lifestyle they were now enjoying, they suffered from low self-worth as they looked forward to uninterrupted days of housework or idleness. The majority of new housewives in the 1950s were women in their teens; more women married at age eighteen than at any other age.[3] For American culture, these allegedly fulfilled, career-averse wives symbolized a stable domestic lifestyle.

But the media in many ways originated the problematic messages about fulfillment and consumerism. *Woman's Day,* which was the official magazine of A & P supermarkets, directly linked a consumer mentality with feminine values by associating women's daily priorities with brand-name (A & P) food shopping for the family. Television shows like "Father Knows Best" and "Ozzie and Harriet" featured additional role models of competent and glamorous Moms.

Formica advertisements in the 1940s always featured women. "Mrs. America" (1948) and other storybook wives narrated their "personal" experiences of choosing and living with Formica laminates. The storytelling strategy bonded values of womanly "good taste" with domestic values of beauty and taste. In furniture showrooms, salesmen encouraged customers to "stop, look and touch" Formica brand products. One press release sent to furniture salesmen in 1949 likened a well-adorned Formica laminate counter to a girl wearing makeup who lures men away from her unmadeup competitors. "Just as a neat hair-do, good looking clothes and the right amount of make-up are assets which a modern girl cannot be without, so Formica counter cards, labels, chip books and colorful literature are the assets needed at the point-of-sale."

The theme of girlish enhancement that pervaded Formica sales literature reflected the popular appeal of a naive, female exuberance that lasted through the 1960s.

6-15
The image of a Formica Girl wearing a giant polka dot minidress appeared frequently in Formica laminate advertisements of the 1960s.

6-16
An advertisement from the early 1950s featured a woman and her Formica-laminate-clad table. Back from the factory assembly lines after World War II, wives and moms became more glamorous in their brighter, more colorful dining rooms.

6-17
This promotional photograph for wood-grain laminates plays on the contrast between the masculine look of a hard-edged, vertical wood-grain application and the seductive look of a 1970s vamp perched on top of a stool.

6-18
This interior of a converted Douglas DC-3 airplane (ca. 1949) featured an extensive use of Realwood Formica laminate on walls, tables, ceiling, bulkheads, wainscoting, cabinets, and luggage compartments. There was more Formica laminate used in this plane interior than any other material.

6-19
Following in the footsteps of the packaged kitchen, the Vanitory was designed to eliminate early morning bathroom traffic in style.

6 | 19

WOOD GRAINS

The modern wood-grain laminate entered Formica product lines in the late forties, when Luxwood, a photographically reproduced wood grain, was introduced to the consumer market. A pattern that evoked ideas of both nature and tradition, it was instantly popular. As diner historian Richard Gutman has pointed out, wood grains were applied as the thematic material in almost every "colonial diner," covering counters, walls, fake beams, and wagon wheels. The setting of the American past, as least as far as architectural interiors were concerned, was housed in wood grains.

But this investment in tradition, and to a certain extent nostalgia for the American colonial and pioneering past, did not alone account for the ubiquity of wood grains.

The wood-grain Formica laminate-covered furniture found in suburban homes during the postwar years replaced many pieces of furniture that were made of actual wood. The logic behind this was not only the consumption of the novel, but also a kind of subscription to the idea of progress. Formica laminate was a versatile material that came in every shade and color. It was shiny, easy to clean, resistant to scratching, and plastic—a material of the future. In this dual signaling of the look of the past and the vision of the future, wood-grain Formica laminate registered a unique moment of desire during a contradictory time in American consumer culture.

Realizing the significance of Luxwood the moment it was developed, Formica Corporation created new markets for the product. One of the targeted audiences was

The text of a 1955 ad tells how a young wife ("gal") acts silly to get what she wants from her husband:

> Bob was strictly lukewarm on the idea of modernizing my kitchen with Formica.
> He kept putting me off until I fell back on every woman's best weapon—psychology.
> Certain colors bring out the best features in a gal and others do less than nothing for her.
> I learned long ago I should always stay away from blue. I practically dragged Bob into a showroom kitchen with the bluest Formica counter tops you ever saw.
> "This is it," said I.
> "You must be out of your mind," he exploded. "You know darn well any setting we put you in has to be green or red."
> Before he knew what hit him he had "sold" me on the green Formica I had picked out months ago.

By narratively infantilizing the wife into a "gal," these kinds of messages spelled out an updated domestic hierarchy and a new, girlish definition of "the little woman." Almost every household commodity proved capable of being "girlified." In the mid-1950s, Formica introduced the bathroom "Vanitory," described as a "combination vanity and lavatory." The name played on both the alluring "laboratory" approach to housekeeping and the pseudoscience of female beauty. The Vanitory promised that "the bathroom ritual" could be a gracious interlude—"like a girl getting ready for a date"—while also "helping the whole family get places on time."

In 1959 the plasticine belittlement of women gelled with the invention of the *men. Men appeared infrequently in Formica advertisements in the late forties and the fifties (though they were seen in "do-it-yourself" instructional materials). The noted exceptions were ads that featured wood grains.*

While patterns such as Fernglo and Pearl were compared to and associated with domestic feminine beauty, wood-grain patterns were invested with masculine attributes. Part of this is certainly due to wood grains' connotations of tradition and power, but more than that, just as the domain of the home can be compared to the female body, wood grains can be seen, as least in domestic settings, as the realm of the man's body.

In a rare 1953 ad for a Vanitory designed for men titled "Reserved for a Man," no man is represented, but, instead,

a wood-grain-paneled Vanitory with a neutral counter is shown encased in a corner, with the same wood-grain paneling on the walls. On the counter are shaving

6 20

6 21

Barbie Doll, a busty figurine meant to be played with by children. Barbie's interests—fun, home decorating, love, romance—matched those of the fairy-tale wife that Betty Friedan dubbed the "happy housewife heroine."[4] During the 1960s, an ingenue "child-woman" look was popularized by cinema icons like Audrey Hepburn in *Breakfast at Tiffany's* (1961) and by the ultimate fashion waif, Twiggy. A synthetic look for the body and the kitchen remained preferable to the "natural" look up to the mid-1960s, as stretch materials and hair spray popularized a laminate look for the body as well as the home. Formica advertisements cultivated domestic versions of various fashion nymphs.

6-20
Rarely were the Vanitory advertisements aimed at men. When they were, the pattern shown was usually a wood grain.

6-21
Introduced in the fifties, the Vanitory promised to "put your bathroom to work" as a place of leisure.

6-22

6 23

6 24

6 25

6 26

6-22
Barnwood pattern,
1965.

6-23
Tawny Walnut Picwood
pattern, 1965.

6-24
Macassar Ebony
pattern, 1965.

6-25
White Tidewood
pattern, 1965.

6-26
Hacienda Ranchwood
pattern, 1965.

cream, after-shave lotion, cigarettes in an ashtray, and a freshly used washcloth which dangles aesthetically from the edge of the counter. The first line of the text reads: "We show this most masculine Formica Vanitory only to prove a point."

The point is clear. Dad has just finished using his Vanitory. But unlike other Vanitory ads, where the woman (Mom) is usually featured in leisurely rituals of maintaining the bathroom or preening over her own body, Dad is conspicuously absent. What informs us that this is a Vanitory "reserved for a man" are the wood grain, a "most masculine" material, and the residue Dad has left behind after the maintenance of his own body—the residue Mom will probably clean up soon.

Simon Leung

By 1970, Formica ads featured the pseudonatural "Formica Girl," who represented the laminate in a more psychedelically attuned age. By the mid-1970s, Formica Corporation—and other companies rethinking their advertising strategies as a result of the women's movement—feminized its products less. There were no more wives mooning over their green Formica laminate kitchens, or bathing beauties watering Formica laminate flower gardens. Contemporary kitchen advertisements often avoid all sexist associations by showing spaces empty of men or women. The modern-day "gourmet kitchen"—often colorless, always unfrilly—avoids gender associations through its neutral style.

The residue of a century's association dies hard. The Surell "Travelling Tray," designed by Joel Sanders and Karen Van Lengen, third-prize winners of the "From Table to Tablescape" competition (and later exhibition, 1988–1990), is a telling comment on the effect of Formica laminate on the perception of women's roles. The contraption is designed to be "worn" by a woman but weighs too much to be of practical use. Held on the body with metal "suspender" cables, the tray protrudes from the abdomen, in effect sheathing the woman as a sort of walking kitchen counter. By wrapping a woman's body in Formica laminate, the apron-tray stands as a macabre postscript to the theories of nineteenth-century designers. The Travelling Tray literalizes the concept of the house as an extension of woman, and its robotic aspect suggests that technological advancements like Formica laminate merely updated, but didn't change, society's coding of women as homemakers. Formica laminate's changing image illustrates prevailing notions of a woman's role in society—and her shifting priorities of power, cleanliness, sexuality, and morality.

6-27
Twiggy, whose preadolescent physique launched a thousand diets in the 1960s. Media nymphets sold synthetic products of every sort.

6-28
The 1988 Traveling Tray, actually designed for a woman's body. A portable counter-bar, it carries a double-edged message about a woman's image as homemaker.

6-29
Barbie in her Barbie-Q outfit, early 1960s.

6 | 28

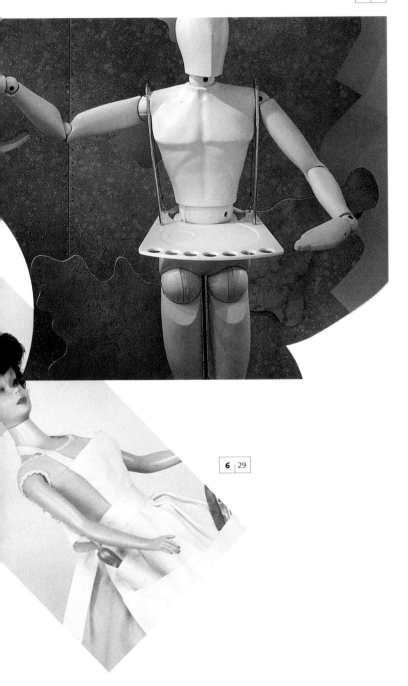

6 | 29

Notes

1   F. Power Cobbe, ''The Final Cause of Woman,'' in *Woman's Work and Woman's Culture*, (London: Butler, 1869), 10-11.

2   This study was done by the staff of the Institute of Motivational Research, Croton-on-Hudson, New York. The institute's consumerism studies for ''business and industry'' were begun in 1945 by Dr. Ernest Dichter and are based on over 300,000 ''depth'' interviews with American housewives. See Betty Friedan, *The Feminine Mystique*, (New York: W. W. Norton & Company, Inc., 1963/Laurel Books, 1983), chapter 9, note 1.

3   This statistic is also from the Institute for Motivational Research, which concluded that 49 per cent of all brides were teenagers during the 1950s. See Friedan, chapter 9.

4   Friedan, *The Feminine Mystique*, chapter 3, [title].

Susan Grant Lewin

FROM MAGICAL TO MUNDANE AND BACK

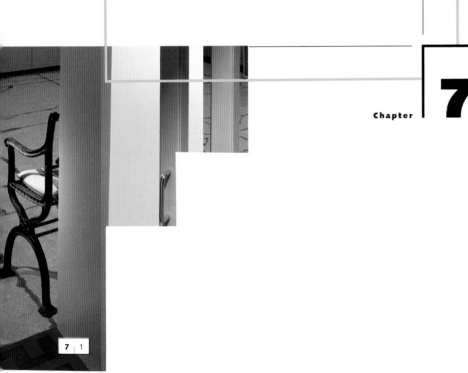

7 1

As Formica brand laminate became ubiquitous, it was in danger of losing the cachet it originally held as a progressive, avant-garde material. In the 1970s it came to be viewed by many as déclassé, even "tacky." Its futuristic, "miracle" image was being tarnished for the same reasons that it covered the coffee shops, kitchens, and bathrooms of America:

low price, durability, and ease of maintenance. The lunch counters of America became paved with it. Everyone wanted it: Armies of suburban housewives relished the fake wood grains and marbles, which naively flaunted their unreal realness.

During the 1950s and 1960s, America had an unending fascination with "man-made" materials, a belief that tomorrow would be better and that Formica laminate represented the future. But in the 1970s, with a growing interest in natural materials, the glitter wore off. A recession mentality made people yearn for permanence.

7-1
Details of Thomas Hall Beeby's colorful ColorCore interpretation of a Greek temple, 1984.
Photos: Karant & Associates.

7-2
Stanley Tigerman, Tête-à-Tête, 1983.
Photo: Hedrich-Blessing, Chicago.

7-3
ColorCore display exhibits the solid-color-through properties of the product, introduced in 1982.

7-4
Stanley Tigerman's design for Formica Corporation's showroom at the Neocon furniture market at the Chicago Merchandise Mart, 1986. The dense labyrinth contained an "object of desire," an elaborate holder for Formica F-chips, at its center.

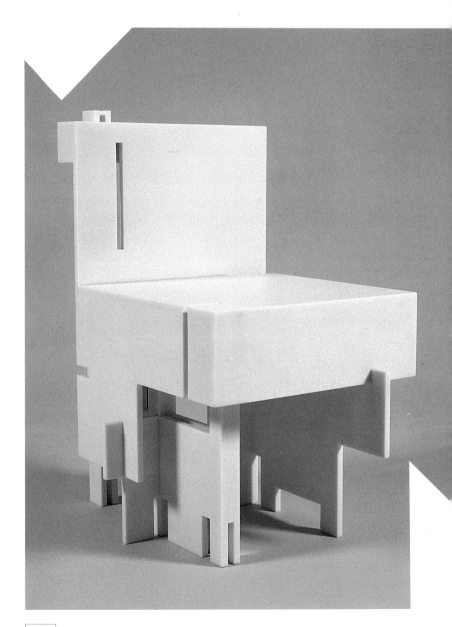

Women wanted to get more in touch with
their roots—through natural childbirth and
breast-feeding for instance—and plastic
laminate just didn't fit in a scenario that
elevated organic farming and downgraded
TV dinners. "Synthetic" and "man-made"
lost the promise they had held at Formica
Corporation's 1964 World's Fair House,
when Formica laminate seemed the ideal
material to surface the world, almost
universal in its appeal.

By the end of the 1970s, the company
realized that it had to reposition its product,
which was suffering from a tainted image.
The first step to recovery was to create a
dialogue with architects and designers, the
product's fastest-growing audience. A
dazzling group of leading architects and

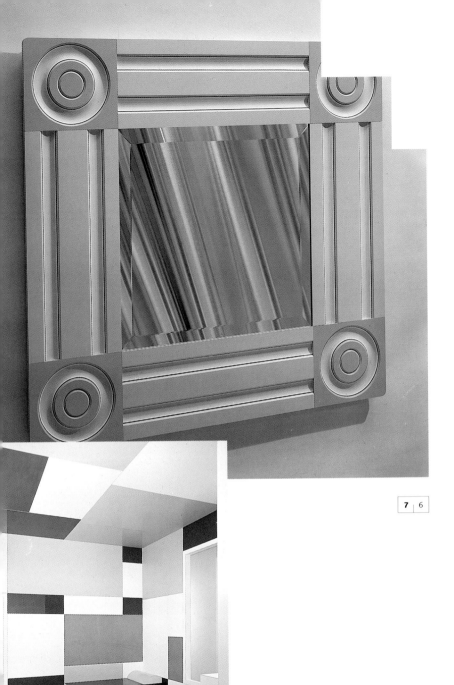

designers from across the country was assembled to form a Design Advisory Board (DAB), representing all of the aesthetic and design vocabularies in use at that time—from the extreme elegance of interior designers John Saladino, Billy McCarty, and Valerian Rybar to the minimalism of Joseph Paul D'Urso and architects Donald Singer and Charles Boxenbaum, to the postmodern leanings of architects William Turnbull, Jr., Richard Hobbs, and Paul Segal, to the pioneering spirit of architect Alan Buchsbaum.

Dexter Design, a team of two New York interior designers—Barbara Schwartz and Barbara Ross—often represented the company. Ross, especially, took to the road, educating the public on Formica laminate's potential as a valid design material. Another architect, Margaret Larcade, of San Antonio, Texas, pushed the parameters of the product.

Ristomatti Ratia, then the creative director of Marimekko in Finland, became the first European member of the board; and Bob Blaich of Philips in the Netherlands became the second. Perhaps Formica Corporation, a global company, already had the idea of someday taking the board international.

Kitchens being a core business, it was deemed essential that at least one member of the board be an expert in commercial and residential kitchens. Charles Morris Mount fit the profile to a T.

Imbued with the 1970s' sensibilities of honesty of materials and letting materials speak for themselves, the board was dismayed by the *faux* side of the company's product line. Plastic should look like plastic, they agreed, and soon, the Design Concepts Collection (the proprietary

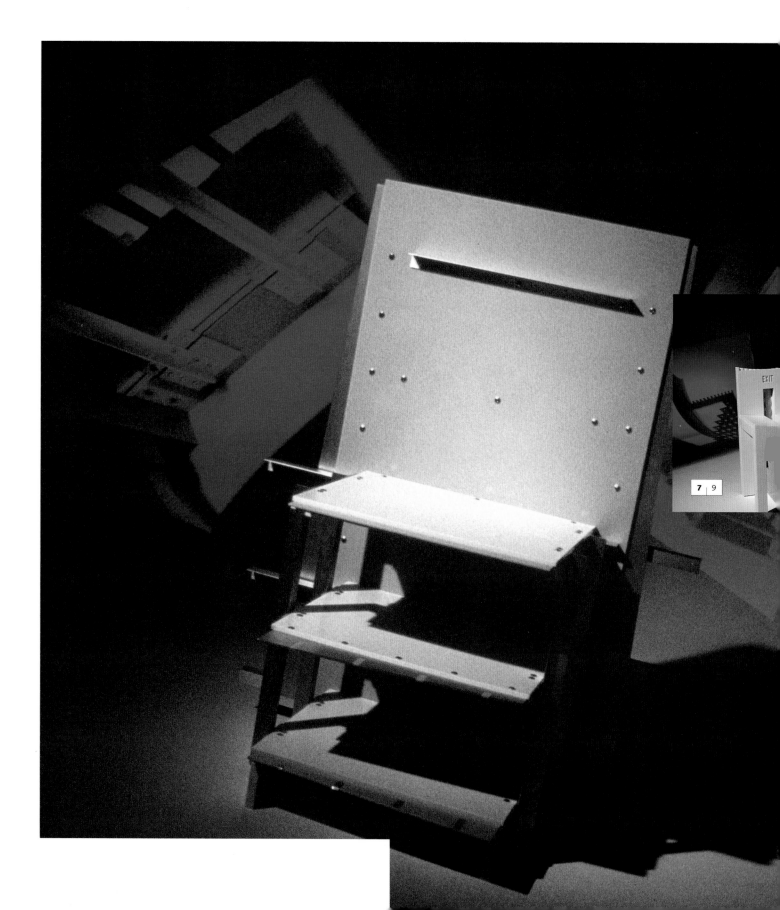

7-8
Peter Rose and
William Steinberg,
Etagère, 1989.
From the company's
Canadian exhibition,
"Prolific Impressions."
Photo: Shin Sugino.

7-9
George Yabu and
Glenn Pushelburg, Exit
Light (chair), 1989.
From the company's
Canadian exhibition,
"Prolific Impressions."
Photo: Shin Sugino.

7-10
David Watkins,
Bracelets, 1986.

technology of which was developed by Formica France) was introduced: a high-lacquer product with geometric designs in contrasting matte finishes that was not imitative in any way. Additionally, the DAB was responsible for convincing Formica Corporation that ColorCore, a surfacing material that had been languishing in research and development, was exactly what the design community wanted—a solid-color-throughout laminate that eliminated the dark lines at seams and corners. It had the look of volume, pure plasticity, and potential for ornamental detail. The DAB also informed the company that design specification would be greatly facilitated if the color line were reorganized with The Color Grid System. This would later become Color + Color, which divided color by family and was organized by Tibor Kalman.

By 1982 the company's consciousness had been sufficiently raised to the point that in-house substitutes for the DAB were possible, and the internal design capacities were augmented with design professionals in touch with both the market and the latest designer concepts.

At this time, ornamentalism and postmodernism were very much in vogue. It was decided that the ColorCore product,

149

Formica Corporation's ace in the hole, a new material with vast decorative design potential, would be given to the leading architects and designers across the United States to experiment with and explore its material potential. Since these pieces would be miniature metaphors for the architects' polemic, it was thought a museum exhibition might be possible.

Actually, the precedent for a museum art exhibition of objects crafted purely in Formica laminate was established in 1970 when New York's Pace Gallery, in cooperation with Formica Corporation, undertook the construction of a room based on Piet Mondrian's original drawings, notes, designs, and color samples. Designed in 1925 for the German art collector and patron Ida Bienert, the library/study was never executed during the artist's lifetime. In 1982 the Mondrian room was shown for the last time at the Akron Art Museum, after touring for more than ten years in New York, Los Angeles, Chicago, and abroad.

"Surface & Ornament" was the first exhibition conceived to demonstrate the possibilities of ColorCore as a design material. Architect Emilio Ambasz, the former curator of design and architecture at the Museum of Modern Art, was commissioned to create the "Call for Entries" announcement poster for "Surface & Ornament," to announce what many consider the benchmark exhibition employing design "celebrities." This interdisciplinary group created conceptual objects that are often cited as emblematic of the 1980s.

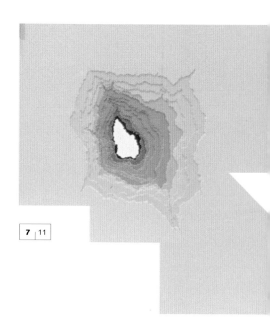

7 | 11

When the exhibit opened in 1983 at Neocon, the design trade exposition at Chicago's Merchandise Mart, in a space designed by Michael Donovan of Donovan & Greene (Formica Corporation's ad agency at that time), it gradually became apparent why the ten invited entrants had been chosen. It was important that the show demonstrate the pluralism within American design. It was also important to tap designers noted for exploration of materials—designers such as Frank O. Gehry, James Wines, and Alison Sky of SITE. Following the Modernist tradition were Helmut Jahn, Emilio Ambasz, Lella and Massimo Vignelli, and Milton Glaser, the last three being the premier graphic designers of the time.

Ward Bennett was selected for his preëminence in furniture design, having distinguished himself as the sole designer for Brickel Furniture and Textiles for twenty-two years. As proponents of postmodernism, the founding fathers of the movement, Robert Venturi and Charles Moore, used ColorCore as a vehicle for both historicism and ornamentalism. The group touched on practical issues as well as on questions of style.

Frank O. Gehry's fish and snakes of chipped, triangular ColorCore shards became legend. In 1988 Mildred Friedman organized Gehry's one-man exhibit at the Walker Art Center, Minneapolis (it later traveled to the Whitney Museum, New York, and to the Museum of Contemporary Art, Los Angeles), which included an unforgettable school of glowing ColorCore fish. The Frank Gehry "Ryba" (fish), along with SITE's multilayered and sandblasted "Door" were also shown at the Whitney's "High Styles: Twentieth-Century American Design" show in 1986. ColorCore had clearly broken beyond the barriers of the trade.

Stanley Tigerman's "Tête-à-Tête," in which ColorCore was curved, and Robert Venturi's "Greek Revival Mirror," which brilliantly demonstrated the creation of ornament through subtraction, quickly changed the design community's view of the company and its products. Invitations poured in from leading museums around the world. Since Formica Corporation is a global company with seven factories around the world, it readily accepted. The exhibit traveled to the Boilerhouse Gallery at the Victoria and Albert Museum, London; the Castello Sforzesco, Milan (where the show was renamed "Design: USA"); the National Museums of Modern Art in Kyoto and Tokyo; and the Poliforum Sequieros in Mexico City.

As writer Martin Filler commented in his essay for the catalogue accompanying the final showing of "Surface & Ornament" in 1986 at Cincinnati's Contemporary Art Center: "The uncommonly high level of quality" and the different results were due to the fact that:

> . . . the invitees were given free rein to determine what they wanted to create, without concern for the marketplace. . . . They were not subject to the restrictions commonplace when inexperienced designers come face to face with what is economically feasible when a commercial, profitable product is the goal.[1]

The "magic secret" of "Surface & Ornament," according to writer Kenneth Brozen in a 1985 cover story in *Interiors,* was "its mythic cheek and suggestive flights."[2]

As the show traveled around the world, pieces by leading architects and designers in a host country were added to the core exhibition. Thus, at the Boilerhouse show, British design talents such as Eva Jiricna and Rodney Kinsman contributed to the exhibition, while in Japan, Arata Isozaki and Shiro Kuramata, two of the most distinguished names in Japanese architecture and design, created new pieces for the exhibition at the Kyoto and Tokyo museums of modern art. A group of young up-and-coming French designers enhanced the showing at the Grand Palais in Paris, while another group of well-known Taiwanese designers exhibited pieces when the show reached Taipei, Formica Corporation's main manufacturing arm in the Far East. The show then traveled to Hong Kong and finished in Singapore before returning to the Contemporary Art Center in Cincinnati.

After the five-year tour, each piece in the show went to a leading museum to be included in its permanent collection. No fewer than four were acquired by the Chicago Art Institute; the Venturi mirror went to New York's Metropolitan Museum; Gehry's "Ryba" to the Museum of Contemporary Art, Los Angeles; and SITE's "Door" to the Deutsches Architekturmuseum in Frankfurt. Ambasz's desk went to the Grand Rapids Museum, where Ambasz had previously developed a controversial remodeling scheme.

Simultaneous with the reëmergence of architects as product designers for interiors was the groundswell of the art-furniture movement. Master craftsmen and -women and cabinetmakers were anxious to use new materials, especially ones that lent themselves to the possibility of color as well as richness of detail and ornament—like the ColorCore product. Creating one-of-a-kind furniture that gave the public an alternative to already expensive production furniture made this the ideal direction for the new product.

In a joint project between the Gallery at Workbench—a national chain of contemporary furniture shops—and Formica Corporation, nineteen of the brightest and best craftsmen and -women were selected, taught about the properties of ColorCore, and then invited to create a unique furniture design.

Upon seeing the show of evocative virtuoso pieces at the Workbench Gallery in New York, the Renwick's then director, Lloyd Herman, initiated a national two-year tour at the Renwick Gallery in Washington, D.C., in May 1985, which then traveled

7-12
Lella and Massimo Vignelli, <u>Broken Length,</u> 1983.
Photo: Hedrich-Blessing, Chicago.

7-13
A2Z, <u>Eye Dazzler #1 and #2,</u> 1986.
Rugs made of ColorCore and Formica laminate.
Photo: Levon Parian.

7-14
Thomas Hall Beeby, Formica showroom, Chicago Merchandise Mart, 1984.
Photo: Karant & Associates.

7 | 14

under the auspices of the Smithsonian Institution Traveling Exhibition Services (S.I.T.E.S.).[3]

Formica Canada staged a design competition for Canadian pieces to accompany the exhibit when it reached the Musée des Arts Décoratifs in Montreal. The work of the winners was also exhibited at the Contemporary Arts Center in Cincinnati.

Concurrent with these two exhibits was "Surface and Edge," a ColorCore show of leading international art jewelers such as David Watkins, Wendy Ramshaw, Thomas Gentille, and Pavel Opočenský, which made several stops, including the Edinburgh Festival in 1987. Initially invited to explore the new laminate's potential for jewelry, these artists have since confirmed the validity of ColorCore, and later Surell (see below), by continuing to work in these products. A case in point is David Watkins, who in 1989 had a major show at New York's Helen Drutt Gallery with a group of minimalist neck rings that combined ColorCore with other materials.

For each exhibition and accompanying opening, or each event like the Formica Lecture Series at The Architectural League of New York (featuring such speakers as the late Arthur Drexler, director of Architecture and Design at the Museum of Modern Art, and British architect James Stirling), and for symposia on subjects such as "Building the New Museum" and "Architecture and Global Culture," major graphic design talent was enlisted to design posters, invitations, and catalogues.

Among the graphic design talents employed during the 1980s and '90s were Michael Beirut of Vignelli Associates, whose Architectural League poster for Arthur Drexler landed in the Museum of Modern Art's poster collection. Later, firms like Bonnell Design Associates, New York, were commissioned to design the company's annual report.

During the mid-1980s, Formica developed a product competitive with DuPont's Corian called Surell, a solid surfacing material. Again, an exhibit and design competition was devised to tap into its material qualities. A dense yet translucent material, Surell lent itself to carving and polishing, qualities exciting to industrial designers, architects, and artists. An emerging graphic design firm, Drenttel Doyle Partners, of New York, was enlisted to handle the graphic presentation of the exhibition, "From Table to Tablescape," when it traveled to Chicago, Minneapolis,

San Francisco, and New York. (As the show traveled, Kelly & Lehn in Kansas City and Robert Probst in Cincinnati offered alternative graphic images for the show.)

Among the fifteen young interdisciplinary firms that participated in "From Table to Tablescape," five design teams chose transparency as the theme of their presentation. Even though Eric Owen Moss, UKZ (Simon Ungers, Laszlo Kiss, and Todd Zwigard), Fred Schwartz and Ross Anderson, Mark Simon, and French designer Patrick Naggar of New York and Paris all worked with this idea to develop lighting fixtures, the results were surprisingly different.[4] After its dramatic opening at the 333 Gallery, Chicago, located in the dazzling Kohn Pedersen Fox building at 333 Wacker, it traveled to Minneapolis and San Francisco with an installation by Mark Mack.

7-15
Charles Moore, <u>Corner Cupboard</u> (detail), 1983.

7-16
Sheila Klein, <u>Water Palace</u>, 1988.

7-17
Dan Friedman, <u>Fountain</u>, 1988.

7 | 15

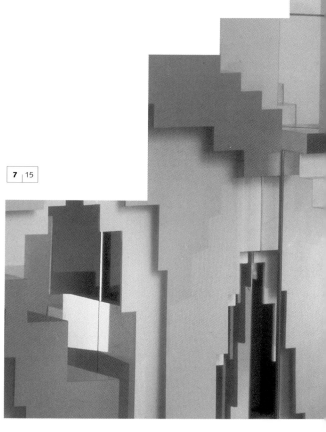

7 | 16

7 | 17

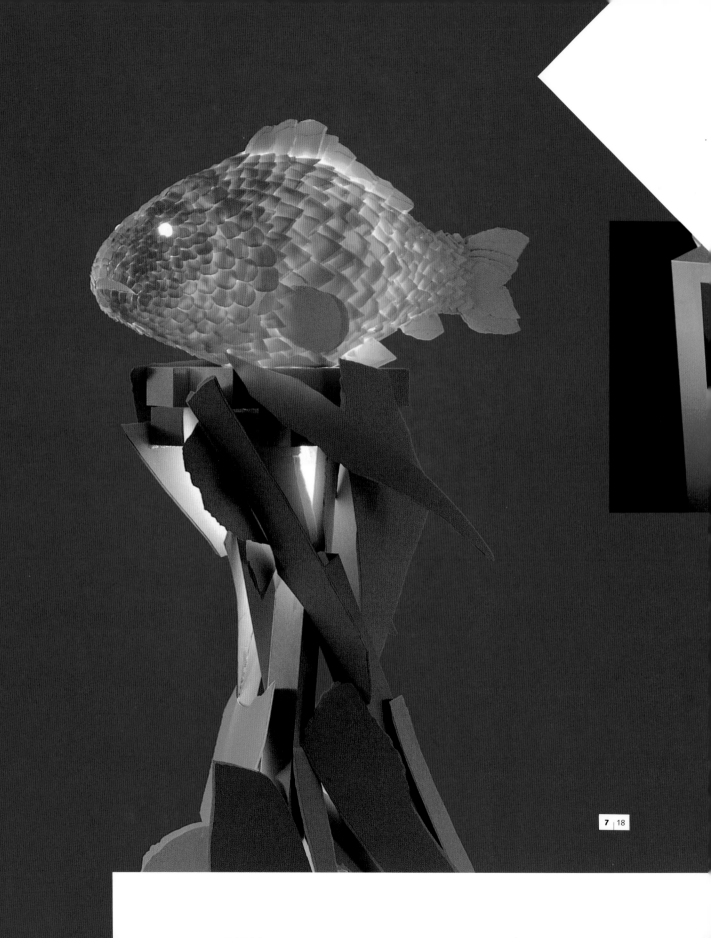

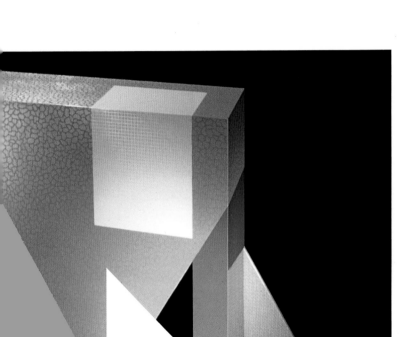

7 | 19

individual works from this exhibition went on to grace the permanent collections of such major American museums as the Metropolitan Museum of Art, Los Angeles County Museum of Art, the Brooklyn Museum, Atlanta's High Museum of Art, the Grand Rapids Art Museum, Yale University Art Gallery, and the Virginia Museum of Fine Arts. The idea of making Formica laminate products the subject of an entire studio class for a semester was also a first at the Kansas City Art Institute.

Inspired by this success, Formica Canada mounted a delightful exhibition of Surell objects at the Royal Ontario Museum. Participants in this show included architects Peter Rose and William Steinberg of Montreal, interior designers Glenn Pushelberg and George Yabu of Toronto, and graphic designer Del Terrelonge, also of Toronto. The collection was later donated as a gift to the Royal Ontario Museum as part of a permanent exhibit on the evolution of plastic as a material for design.

When the exhibit opened in Chicago, the design community saw for the first time the 12-foot-high "Water Palace," designed by Los Angeles artist Sheila Klein, formerly of A2Z. Klein, with the help of Ries Niemi, Norman Millar, and Gale McCall, used Surell to create this monumental sculpture, which also functions as an entirely self-contained and recirculating fountain with three waterways. The fountain, a witty

It was in December 1989, however, that the exhibit picked up momentum. Kansas City designer Thomas Lehn placed the show in a colorful environment at the Kansas City Art Institute's Charlotte Crosby Kemper Gallery—a setting that connected the objects to actual applications. The show traveled in this form to the University of Cincinnati's Tangeman Fine Arts Gallery in February 1990, and Soho's Gallery 91, specializing in art furniture, served as the perfect venue for a New York showing beginning in October 1990 during the Designer's Saturday market week. The

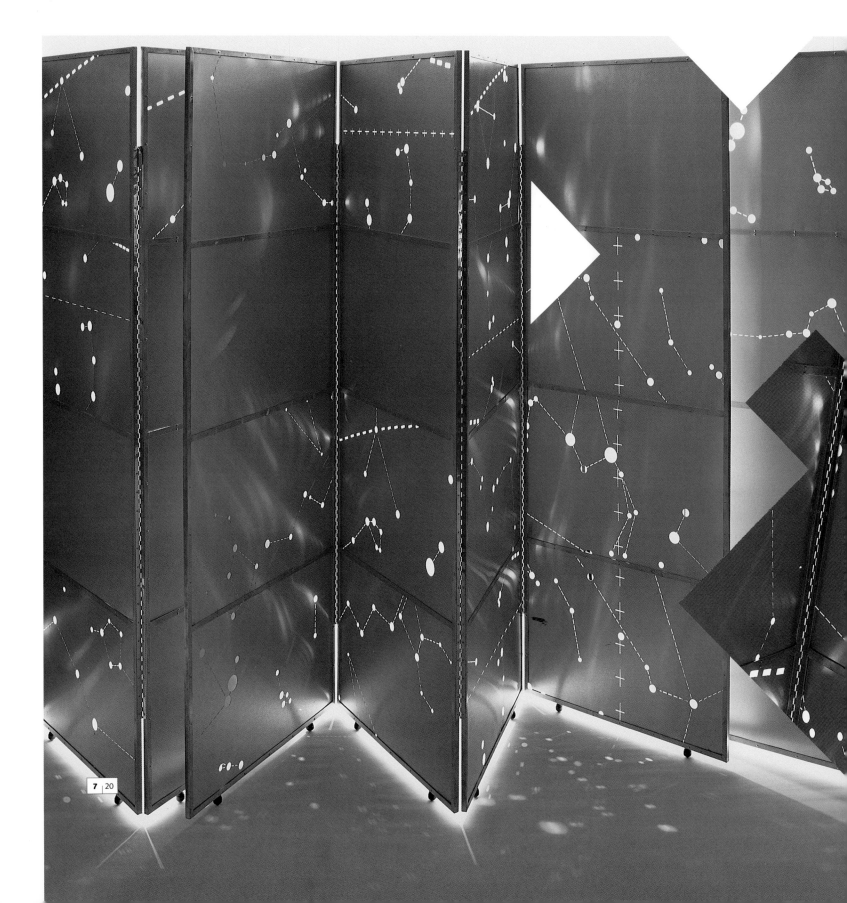

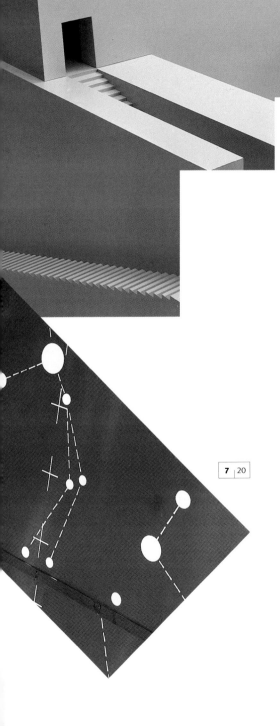

7-20
Bausman·Gill
Associates, Folding
Screen, 1990.
This monumental screen
(8 × 30 feet) is made of
Brushed Aluminum
Metal from Formica
Corporation's 1990
International Collection
of Metal Laminates.
Photo: Elliott Kaufman.

7-21
Lewis & Clark
(Jim Lewis and
Clark Ellefson),
Temple Chair
(detail), 1983.
This piece took
first prize in the
"Surface & Ornament"
open competition.
Photo: Hedrich-Blessing,
Chicago.

reinterpretation of the classical public sculpture, features an inventive assemblage of overflowing bathtubs, vanity sinks, and shower bases, stacked in a pyramid configuration with three cascading waterfalls. It would later find a permanent home in 1989 at the Bass Museum of Art in Miami Beach.

Exhibitions were far from the only strategy Formica Corporation was employing to reposition its image. The interior of its small, but effective, Chicago showroom took major design awards at Neocon for the years that the company exhibited there (1982–86). "Surface & Ornament" was the company's first major display in Chicago. It was followed in successive years by a ColorCore interpretation of a Greek temple by Yale architecture dean Thomas Beeby of Hammond, Beeby & Babka, Chicago, and architect Stanley Tigerman's three-dimensional walk-through grid with the object of desire—an elaborate holder for F-chips (Formica laminate samples)—at the center. This was yet another powerful statement of the company's design commitment.

In 1985 the newly constructed, but not yet installed, office of Formica Corporation's then CEO, Gordon Sterling, designed by Cranbrook Academy's design co-chairs, Katherine and Michael McCoy, filled the Neocon space, after being exhibited at WestWeek in Los Angeles. This was the third in a series of experimental interiors created by the McCoys and their students at the Cranbrook Academy.

The first collaboration between Formica Corporation and Michael McCoy took place in 1983 when an office for an automotive executive was created in the

Beylerian furniture showroom in New York. The second one occurred at the International Design Center, New York (IDCNY), in 1984 where Cranbrook students created a computer-aided design office. Both were the subjects of major articles in *Interiors* magazine as part of their "Design Initiative" program. No wonder Gordon Sterling invited the McCoys to demonstrate that ColorCore was the appropriate material for a CEO's office— especially if one were the CEO of Formica Corporation.

The material vocabulary for designers relaxed in the eighties. Liberated from kitchens and coffee shops, plastic laminates found entirely new applications. A new audience was introduced to the wonder felt by postwar generations when confronted by such synthetic substances as Formica laminate.

An example of the new "chic" use of Formica laminate in restaurants was the "Cafe Millennium" exhibition at WestWeek at the Pacific Design Center in Los Angeles in March 1990. The "Cafe Millennium," a temporary restaurant, was the realization of students at Art Center College of Design in Pasadena. Art Center student Ken Jacobson, whose design was selected from several proposals, created a vertical structure that filled the atrium at the Pacific Design Center. In a similar vein, New York's Bausman · Gill Associates dazzled audiences at Designer's Saturday 1990 with a constellation screen made of Brushed Aluminum metals from The International Collection.

On the advertising front, Keith Goddard of Studio Works was the designer selected to create the company's graphic image for the nineties (by turning the

7 | 22

7 | 23

7 | 25

7 | 26

7 | 27

7 | 24

7-22
Patrick Naggar, Hypnos
Sleep Light, 1988.

7-23
Billie Tsien,
Glass Screen, 1988.

7-24
Eric Owen Moss,
One Wilshire, 1988.

7-25
Mark Simon,
Breeze, 1988.

7-26
UKZ, The Globus Lamp,
1988.

7-27
Frederic Schwartz and
Ross Anderson,
Pattern on Pattern,
1988.

161

famous anvil *F* on its side), and to promote
for the first time the fact that this was
indeed a global company. The idea of
a global Formica Corporation was
promoted via a sweepstakes poster, which
gave the concept a delightfully irreverent
send-off with a global volleyball floating in
F-chips (as Formica laminate samples are
known throughout the world).

The goal was always to be on the
lookout for young, emerging talent to
supplement the solid work created by
Phyllis Chillingworth of Chillingworth/
Radding. Siebert Design of Cincinnati came
to light in a conversation with Michael
Beirut of Pentagram. Their eroded collages
and primitive motifs were perfect in
illustrating the company blockbuster
collection of 1991, "Formations."

While Formica Corporation continues to make new commitments to design and develop new, sophisticated audiences, older generations continue to cherish their memories of Formica laminate. During the Formica Corporation 75th-Anniversary Media Tour, as Creative Director I made television appearances across the country. Television hosts were even singing "Happy Birthday" to Formica with nostalgia in their voices for this product that reminded them of their youth. In each city, the major metropolitan daily followed with an article documenting the anniversary with tales of the golden years of the 1950s and '60s.

The following passage is a favorite of mine for its utter enthusiasm and nostalgia for the product that seemed so "magical" in the 1950s. It was written by the *Kansas City Star*'s George Gurley, Jr., and inspired by his memories of the impact of Formica laminate on his family in the 1950s:

> It was a magical, watershed event. . . . No longer would Mom have to slave away for hours trying to remove nasty stains . . . from the worn oilcloth. . . . We were simple folk back then. A homely product such as Formica could thrill us so. . . . Formica brought our family together. In those days before television claimed our souls, we considered it the highest entertainment to gather in the kitchen and watch Mom demonstrate the amazing properties of her new counter top. We watched in horror as she audaciously emptied a bilious mixture of noxious fluids over the immaculate, gold-flecked surface. We let out a terrific cheer when with an effortless swipe of the cloth she suavely removed the nasty mess. Then Mom would leap into the air and spin like a ballerina, cleaving the air with a vicious karate chop and letting out an ear-splitting primal scream. And we would rise in jubilation, swaying with rapture, and break out into a chorus of spontaneous song: "Formica, Formica, oh how we like ya." (Sung to the tune of "To market, to market to buy a fat pig.")[5]

Could anyone ever doubt the magic of Formica laminate again?

7-28
Michael and Katherine
McCoy's ColorCore
office for Formica
Corporation Chairman
Gordon Sterling. The
office was exhibited
at WestWeek 1985.

7-29
Ken Jacobson's Cafe
Millennium was
designed as a temporary
restaurant at the
Pacific Design Center,
Los Angeles, during
the WestWeek
market, 1990.

Notes

1   Martin Filler,
"Surface & Ornament," in
Surface & Ornament
catalogue (Cincinnati:
Contemporary Arts Center,
1986), 8.

2   Kenneth Brozen,
"Working It Out," *Interiors*
(September 1985), 198.

3   The show traveled to
twelve additional cities
between October 1985 and
November 1987: Mobile,
Alabama; Kutztown,
Pennsylvania; Montreal,
Quebec; Tampa, Florida;
Midland, Michigan; Little
Rock, Arkansas; Boca
Raton, Florida; Colorado
Springs, Colorado; Dayton,
Ohio; Laguna Beach,
California; Toronto,
Ontario; and Grand Rapids,
Michigan.

4   Other participants
included Dan Friedman,
New York; Steven Holt &
Michael Pinkus, New York;
Mark Mack, San Francisco;
Brian Murphy, Pacific
Palisades, California;
George Ranalli, New York;
Jesse Reiser & Nanako
Umemoto, New York; Peter
Shire, Los Angeles; Bruce
Tomb and John Randolph,
San Francisco; Billie Tsien,
New York; and Tucker
Viemeister, New York.

5   George H. Gurley,
Jr., "Miracle Merely
Mundane," *Kansas City
Star* (5 November, 1988),
2:1.

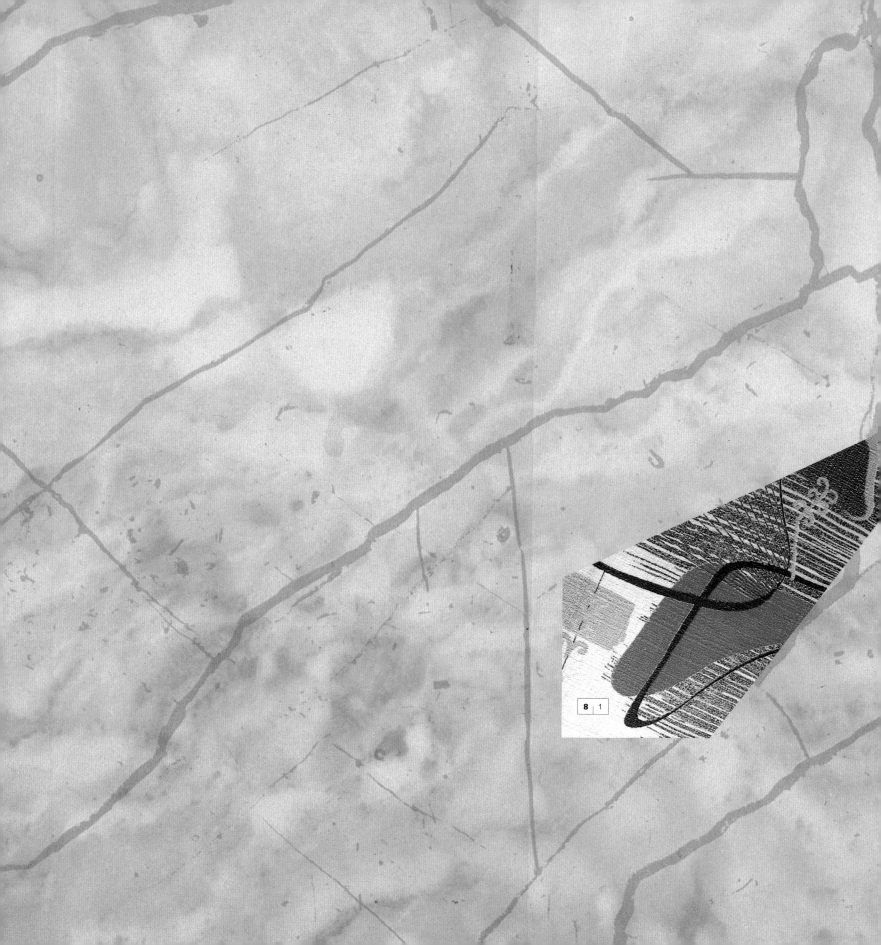

8 | 1

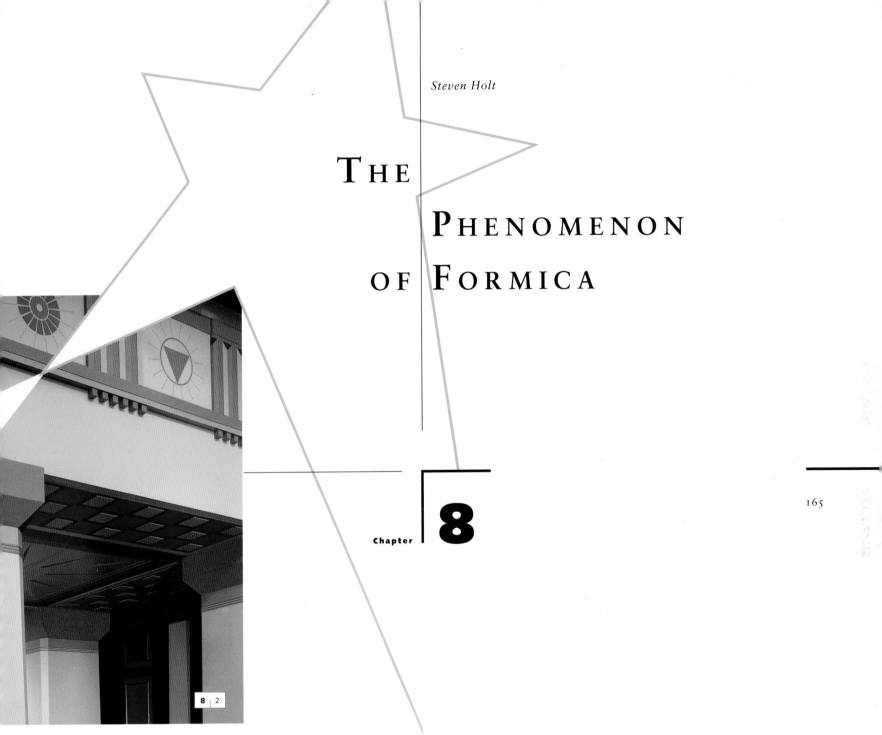

Steven Holt

THE
PHENOMENON
OF FORMICA

Chapter 8

8 | 2

It is hard to imagine something more resistant to both stain and to inspection than Formica laminate. To a mid- to late-twentieth-century eye, it appeared to be something so resolutely normal that there was simultaneously no need for a history and no possible cause for a critique. But to our rapidly mutating, late-twentieth- and early twenty-first-century eyes, the realm of invisible behavior that Formica laminate has occupied is now of extreme interest, precisely because it is the place that both tells us more about ourselves and that provides a composite archaeological rendering of the most recent era.

The phenomenon of Formica laminate, approached philosophically, reveals the profound depths that even the thinnest of surfaces can offer. Up through the 1970s, the laminate achieved the quality of an essence, became a kind of Barthesean, historyless substance alternating between commercial and residential use. Twenty years ago it was as if Formica laminate were an empty vessel into which we poured meaning; it depended upon context for its

8-1
1950s pattern.
Photo: Moyra Davey.

8-2
Detail of Thomas Hall Beeby's ColorCore interpretation of a Greek temple.
Photo: Karant & Associates.

8-3
Venturi, Rauch and Scott Brown, Signs of Life: Symbols in the American City, 1976.
From the exhibition, "Suburban Home Life: Tracking the American Dream," 1989.
Photo courtesy of Whitney Museum of American Art, Fairfield County.

8-4
Richard Hamilton, Just what is it that makes today's home so different, so appealing? 1956.
Photo courtesy of The Institute for Contemporary Art.

8-5
Stephen Shore, Long Island, New York, 1975.
A suburban scene where the sidewalks are immaculate, the inhabitants invisible, and time stands still.

associations. Its meaning appeared to come from what was around it rather than what it was; its value appeared to come from *how* it was employed rather than *why* it was employed.

To both the design practitioner and the journalist of this time, Formica laminate was part of a much larger and more general postwar blessing of plenty that was quickly accepted and little questioned. Because Formica laminate encouraged quick construction for builders and symbolized middle-class modernity (and easy cleaning) for homeowners, it made sense to build rather than investigate. Given the laminate's success, there was little incentive to examine what the material was and what it might do besides cover counters.

It was only once laminate was recognized as a material in its own right that it began to have a history, and, not coincidentally, began to be transformed as a material. The shift from a Modern to a postmodern condition encouraged a rethinking of the material with respect to such aspects as color and form, but underlying even this was a sometimes radical, always present reëxamination of materials of all types. As the postmodern approach rose into prominence, Formica laminate was catapulted into a newfound role as a material of particular appropriateness for its time; it was singled out, for example, in *Art & Design's* special issue, "The Post-Modern Object."

The event that relaunched Formica laminate's prominence in the design arena was the company's self-sponsored "Surface & Ornament" exhibition of 1983. This exhibit, named by Emilio Ambasz and designed in the largest sense by Formica Corporation's newly selected Creative

8-6
**Jeff Koons, <u>Naked,</u>
1988.**
The "postmodern artist"
celebrates the mundane
in an artificial manner,
questioning definitions
of "art."

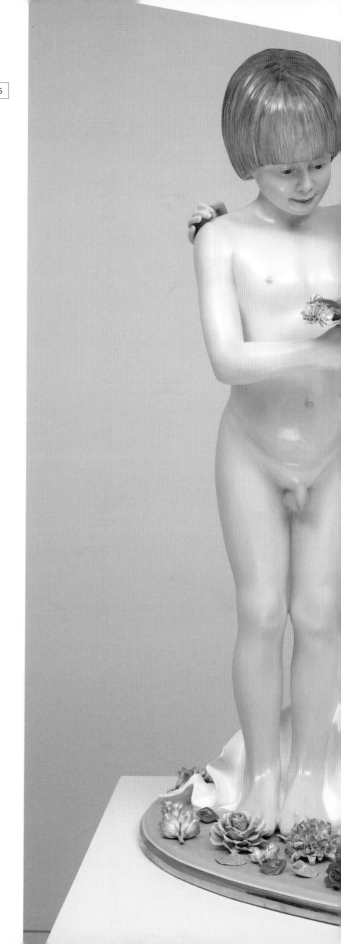

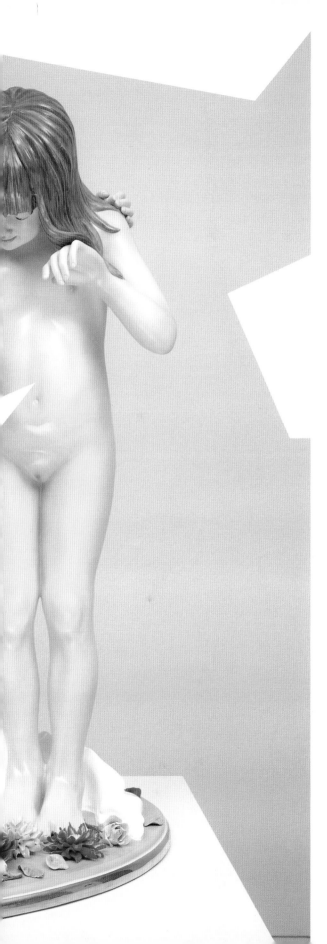

Director, Susan Grant Lewin, celebrated the release of a new product called ColorCore, but the effects of "Surface & Ornament" went far beyond a normal product introduction. Formica laminate of all types began to be looked at in ways that were unimaginable just a few years earlier. This questioning manifested itself in a range of startling work, including Frank Gehry's shattered fish-shaped lights, Stanley Tigerman's wavy seating for two, and SITE's punctured, delayering door.

This date also approximates a cultural transition, a shift from an industrial to an information-based society, from a concern solely with production of objects to a broader focus on the production of meaningful products. Work in Formica laminate reflects this change; it becomes aware and self-referential and reflects lessons from pop art and the "me generation." As the postmodern condition has come to be the norm rather than the subversive agent it was fifteen years ago, laminate has come to be viewed as possessive of its own meanings and inherent associations, its own strangely and strongly prosaic qualities that are ready to be drawn upon by the artist, craftsman or -woman, designer, or architect. Seen and probably used by each of us every day, it is a material about which we know more than we ever have. But laminate is still a mystery in many ways. What television game show queries its contestants as to the nuances of plastic laminates? What best seller shows off its jet-set cast's deep cultural awareness by having them ask each other about their favorite counter tops?

Even if laminate isn't the subject of common conversation, it has enjoyed a unique rise to stardom. It has become a creative as well as a functional material, a covering for many surfaces but also a kind of artifact that in many ways seems uniquely American in its identity. Formica laminate represents a series of qualities we as Americans aspire to, and in fact, many think we already exemplify. In examining these qualities, can we, to paraphrase cultural historian Gaston Bachelard, explain the phenomenological flowering of Formica laminate in America by looking at its "fertilizer?"[1]

The search for "fertilizer" begins in the 1950s, arguably the most fertile decade of the American experience. Clearly, there are striking parallels between the United States of the 1950s and that of the 1980s. In both periods, we find an American preference for objects that do more, even if that means not working as well, so that they can communicate something of themselves more fully. In both periods, we discover groundbreaking work done in color, form, pattern, and research into primitive aesthetics. (In the 1950s it might have been a generalized vision of African warriors; in the 1980s it was specific patterns from tribes like the Ndebele.) Experimentation took place at greater-than-normal levels. Also, everything from objects to architecture reflected an expanded concern for convenience, comfort, and leisure, and questions concerning the aesthetics of plenty and issues of style were present at the smallest and largest of built scales.

Formica laminate's politics in any decade resided in the fact that it was witty without being pretentious or overbearing; it was decorative to the degree required and no more; it democratically offered the consumer multiple product choices; and it had a visible effect on the look of other

8-7
The Carlyle Hotel, in Miami Beach's Art Deco historic district. *Photo courtesy of Robert G. Kuebler.*

8-8
A Shaker rocker exemplifies a functional, unadorned strain in American design.

8-9
Interior of a Boeing 707, designed by Walter Dorwin Teague in 1955. Formica laminate panels became ubiquitous in airplane interiors in the 1950s.

things, including kitchens as a whole and the home. Just as accurately repeatable words, pictures, and music mutated the idea of what culture stood for with the advent of mass-production techniques, so, too, the introduction of Formica laminate on a mass level in the 1950s created an expanded, expendable forest of signs and symbols.

This multitude of signs and symbols, as well as the multitude of new materials and new construction techniques, began to raise questions about the distinction between what we consider artificial (always considered to be "fake") and what natural (always considered to be "true"), questions that are particularly poignant when asked about an artificial material such as Formica laminate. The roots of this distinction go back centuries, but the contemporary discussion of the subject also finds its origins in the mid-fifties with the advent of a "superconsumerist" understanding of art, design, and even daily life—at the same time that the wholesale replacement of enamel took place and that Formica laminate became the table- and counter top material of choice because of its heat-resistant and hard-wearing properties.

As Raymond Guidot has noted, the 1950s marked the end of "refined culture."[2] Exuberance was everywhere. The harshness and destitution of the war turned people away from purely functional, rigor-laden design. But the changes that took place were not confined to design alone. As Kenneth Helphand has remarked, "In the mid-1950s, our physical as well as our social environment changed; the contemporary American landscape was born."[3]

Between the efforts of the Federal Housing Administration and the Veteran's

171

Administration, houses were financed, built, and mortgaged to eager buyers under a no-money-down policy. Ownership of houses increased more in the 1950s than it had in the previous 150 years; the upshot was that an inordinate number of counter tops were covered with Formica laminate. The ever-prescient George Nelson was one of the few to look around and ponder. He remarked several decades ago that we live in an ever more synthetic world, a "designed" (that is to say, artificial) culture. By this, Nelson meant that what is around us is less something that is organically grown, and more something that is (like Formica laminate) the combined product of imagination and factory.

As the artificial has become natural to us, we have shifted from the nineteenth-century's "Beaux-Arts" approach to the twentieth-century's "Faux Arts." We see evidence of, and commentary on, this shift everywhere; the line between real and fake is continually blurred: Cindy Sherman's photographic portraits of herself; Barbara Kruger's billboards with reclaimed messages; Haim Steinbach's assemblages of consumer goods (which incidentally always use a wedge shape built of wood and encased in single-color [black, grey, pink, red, etc.] Formica laminates, the ends of which are left open to expose the construction); Mike Bidlo's exhibitions of "Picassos" he himself painted; Robert Palmer's music videos in which models mime musical instruments; the 1940s' American fashion for plastic fruit in real bowls; Umberto Eco's descriptions of the Madonna Inn in San Luis Obispo, California; Robert Abel's special effects. The list stretches to infinity, or at least to the American horizon. Recall J. B. Priestley's

quote, "The fact is that Americans never seem to me to be real people at all," or run into rock singer David Lee Roth's words of wisdom, "The key to this business is sincerity, and when you can fake that you have got it made," and you quickly get the sense that the fake has a special place within the American landscape.

Formica laminate—a material that is always becoming and never being—makes its fakes in truly American style, with exuberance and sincerity. In 1963, for example, Formica produced its Nubian line, which imitated a group of beautiful exotic woods. In a country where having enough isn't ever enough, Formica laminate at least allows for the *image* of having more than one possibly can or should. In its portrayals of already extant and sometimes invented fabrics, metals, stones, and woods of

8 | 10

8 | 11

8 | 10

8-10
Haim Steinbach, 00:05
(1, 3L) (details), 1989.

8-11
Haim Steinbach, Tango
Vigor #3, 1989.

8-12
Ashley Bickerton,
Tormented Self-portrait
(Susan at Arles) #2,
1988.
*Photo courtesy of
Sonnabend Gallery.*

varying preciousness, Formica laminate charts the tension between what is real and looks real, what is real but looks fake, and what is fake and looks fake. Even if we grasp the essential deception that is at the core of Formica laminate right off, it has become so ubiquitous in America that it is nonetheless a trusted, "traditional" home decorating material.

With respect to a philosophy of possessions, two threads run consistently through the American experience, and there are infinite examples of each. The first thread is that of parsimony. Tools, weapons, and high-performance racing machines are maximally minimal; Shaker furniture is direct, pure, and unfettered by ornament; Niels Diffrient's office seating is inspired by a close study of the simplicity of things like canoes and bows and arrows; life at Walden Pond for Henry David Thoreau was unmitigatedly straightforward. All of these examples emphasize singularity of expression, a right, sometimes moralistic, approach to how things should be.

The second thread is the exact opposite: gaudiness. As Robert Venturi phrased it, "messy vitality over obvious unity."[4] Las Vegas, Liberace, and lava lamps. Customized automobiles, the encrusted work of Simon Rodia's Watts Towers and that of hundreds of other obsessed folk artists; Susan Sontag's lauding of "camp"; Miami Art Deco hotels; and the highly colored and patterned furniture of early America. This is the side of plurality, of fetishistic activity by specialist and lay person alike, of kitsch (which Clement Greenberg described as ". . . vicarious experience and faked sensations . . . the epitome of all that is spurious," which sounds like Formica laminate).[5]

The interesting thing is not that these two threads exist, but that they intertwine, interweave, and define much of the American experience. It was not uncommon, for example, for a suburban house of the 1950s and 1960s to have a mink-lined beer opener hanging up in a streamlined, Modernist kitchen, and a Louis XIV television set up in a "colonial" or "Regency-style" living room.

In fact, Formica laminate was a microcosm of the American experience, a paradigmatic example of a product that offered both parsimony and gaudiness, sometimes even within a single sheet. On the parsimonious side, the Formica product was a labor-saving "appliance" in the same sense that a washing machine or any other

device that made cleaning easier was. Formica laminate was also "streamlined," as was much of the decorative arts, furniture, and architecture of the time, which were given cleaner lines and a smoother, functional appearance. The 1950s also saw the introduction of such clean typefaces as Helvetica and Univers, and airplanes were made sleeker, most notably through the efforts of Walter Dorwin Teague's work for Boeing, the company that introduced the 707 in 1955.

The 707 signaled the beginning of the "jet age," and in the same year the release of the "Rock Around the Clock" album by Bill Haley and the Comets launched the rock-and-roll age. In a world where everything was becoming brighter, cleaner, more fun, and newer, Formica laminate fit in perfectly, offering all of these qualities, or

as one ad from the period claimed, "Lucky the mother whose table is Formica topped. No need to scrub—one wipe with a damp cloth and it's clean. It's almost like magic the way this modern laminated plastic banishes work and brings beauty and ease into your home."

While the simplest Formica laminate colors, like off-white, have been the biggest sellers over the years, an array of color and pattern combinations has continuously appeared. Because Formica laminate is essentially a resin-impregnated piece of kraft paper, any colors and patterns are technically possible. Formica laminate can be as loud, obnoxious, and garish as one wants, or as subdued, restrained, and quiet as one needs. It is an American contradiction that all of us live with both the parsimonious and the gaudy, the simple

8-13
Edward Wormley,
Gaming Table, 1964.
An innovator in furniture
design in the 1950s and
'60s, Edward Wormley
used Formica laminates
in many designs.

8-14
Formica laminate plastic
tabletops traveling
between styles—
from antebellum
to 1960s futuristic.

175

8-15
A Vanitory made
of rocks?
A view of the
Cave-man suite of the
Madonna Inn,
San Luis Obispo, CA.
Photo:
Danielle Gustuffson.

8-16
Disneyland, opened in
1955, is a paradise
of simulation.

8-17
The "Big Boy" statues in
front of many Big Boy
restaurants stand against
backgrounds of brick
walls and columns.

and the complex, and it is also an American strength. In a country that had to be invented as well as discovered, this is ultimately the soil from which Formica laminate springs. We live at a time when both approaches are valid, a time when the tension between the real and the fake, the austere and the excessive, and the natural and the artificial, is never resolved and can never be resolved.

More recently, Andrea Branzi has written of our relationship to the artificial. His focus is on how the artificial is integrated into our lives.:

> Up until twenty years ago, the term "normal" meant a sort of adherence to a gray, flat and banal "naturalness." The new normality, on the other hand, can be described as "abnormal": abnormal in the sense that it is profoundly artificial, the outcome of a complex process of inquiry that has overturned the concept of "normality." [6]

Regardless of its application, Formica laminate was a "pop" material in the sense of the term as it was originally coined by Lawrence Alloway. Pop referred not only to collages, paintings, or prints that the artists produced but to the raw material that came before the artistic product. Ads, comics, packages, posters, and new materials, which have a special relationship to the aesthetic trends of the day, have made the laminate a kind of public art for all to enjoy.

Formica laminate has been part of this process of democratization of style, taste, and aesthetics, and it has been used to differentiate areas of components, products, counters, rooms, and even zones within a single room such as the kitchen. It has created the possibility for almost any color to be used in contemporary decoration, and it has made it possible at

8-18
Wichstand coffee shop,
1957, Los Angeles, CA.
*Photo: Jack Laxer
courtesy of Armet, Davis
and Newlove Architects,
Santa Monica, CA.*

8-19
Ship's Westwood, 1958,
Los Angeles, CA.
*Photo courtesy of
Emmett Shipman.*

the same time to indulge in personal rather than mass preferences. As Alan Hess notes in *Googie*, coffee houses completed part of Walter Gropius's dream of a new architecture conceived and used by the masses, one that expressed the high American standard of living and that employed a lot of Formica laminate, although it should be noted that "the forms were not what Gropius expected," as Hess demurely put it.[7]

The enduring lessons of Formica laminate—besides its inevitable connection with the 1950s and icons such as TV dinners, canned beer, Fabulous Pink Camay, and long-finned Cadillacs—are that the surfaces of things merit considerably more attention than they receive; that these surfaces are bearers of social meaning; and that authenticity or genuineness has less significance to most consumers than the relative importance they assign to a given object. The apparent historyless realm of invisible behavior that Formica laminate was thought to occupy several decades ago has proven instead to be a treasure trove of visual calories and historical significance.

Formica laminate, a hyperreal material straight to the core of its artificial center, is a replica that is often better than the real thing, a material unlike anything else ever conjured from the minds of man. If plastic is the material that has defined the twentieth century—and it undoubtedly is—a strong case can be made for Formica laminate being the plastic of plastics. It is naive yet optimistic, youthful and action-oriented, symbolic of superabundance yet capable of irony, in short, a perfect material for late-twentieth-century America.

Such are the power and the scope of the new artificial "abnormal normality" that we cannot imagine our homes (indeed, our lives) without it, and such is the power of certain materials, like Formica laminate, that embody this schizophrenic acceptance of diverse qualities, that we cannot imagine our lives without them, either. Formica laminate is the analogue to bark in the synthetic forests of our contemporary world, the physical corollary to skin on some of our era's most beloved bodies.

If there is a lesson to our time, a message that is both written on the bark of our everyday objects and hidden beneath their skin, it is that things are not necessarily what they seem to be. We are arguably the smartest generation ever, and yet we are fooled all the time. The rain forest we watch on television is a cleverly tracked stage set; the stone in the hotel lobby with the waterfall cascading over its edge is only an inch deep; the person dressed as an elderly woman is actually a graduate student doing field research.

Formica laminate is part of this era's practice of practiced deception. Given the costs of quarried stone and exotic hardwoods, Formica laminate is more than a convenient fiction. It is an appropriate fiction. As Jean Cocteau said of America in 1956, "Your ideal world would be an instantaneous tradition." Formica laminate is a perfect material for this ideal world, not only because it is a thoroughly modern material, but because it is an instantaneous one as well. Barely possessive of depth, the laminate appears to come from nowhere, yet it has only to arrive and it can be set in place, a familiar yet fantastic substance that, depending upon how it is used, can be either precious or nonprecious, and that has subsequently been appreciated by artists like Richard Artschwager since the early

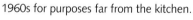

8 | 20

1960s for purposes far from the kitchen.

Formica laminate is a perfect material in Cocteau's sense, a planar analogue to the butler. By never reflecting either world wars or wear and tear, by never showing social concern or cigarette burns, the laminate renders a seamless, eternally consistent world. This is in part because Formica laminate doesn't just solve a design problem, it enriches it. Like Coca-Cola, laminate adds life, but it uses color, texture, and pattern instead of caffeine and sugar.

As architecture and design writer Philip Langdon has noted, laminate was one of the key ways by which color was introduced to coffee shops. Designers were quick to see this potential and often contrasted the artificiality of the laminate with a wall of

natural material (brick or stone), as was
done in the Big Boy restaurants designed by
Armet & Davis. Some coffee shops even
used inlaid laminate in contrasting colors to
define a personal space for each diner,
reinforcing the notion that each person had
his or her own place. As Langdon reports,
the colors most frequently chosen for coffee
shops and Friendly's and Howard Johnson's
restaurants were not restful but were
shades of orange and pink which were
believed to stimulate the appetite and move
customers in and out faster, thus generating
more money as a result of the higher
turnover.

Notes

1   Gaston Bachelard,
The Poetics of Space, trans.
(Boston: Beacon Press,
1964).

2   Kenneth I.
Helphand, "McUrbia: The
1950's and the Birth of the
Contemporary American
Landscape," *Places*, Vol. 5,
No. 2, 40.

3   Ibid.

4   Robert Venturi,
*Complexities and
Contradictions in
Architecture* (New York:
Doubleday, 1966), 22.

5   Clement Greenberg,
"On Kitsch," *Partisan
Review*, Fall 1939, 24.

6   Andrea Branzi,
*Domestic Animals:
Neoprimitive Style*
(Cambridge, MA: M.I.T.
Press, 1987), 3.

7   Alan Hess, *Googie*
(San Francisco: Chronicle
Books, 1985), 95.

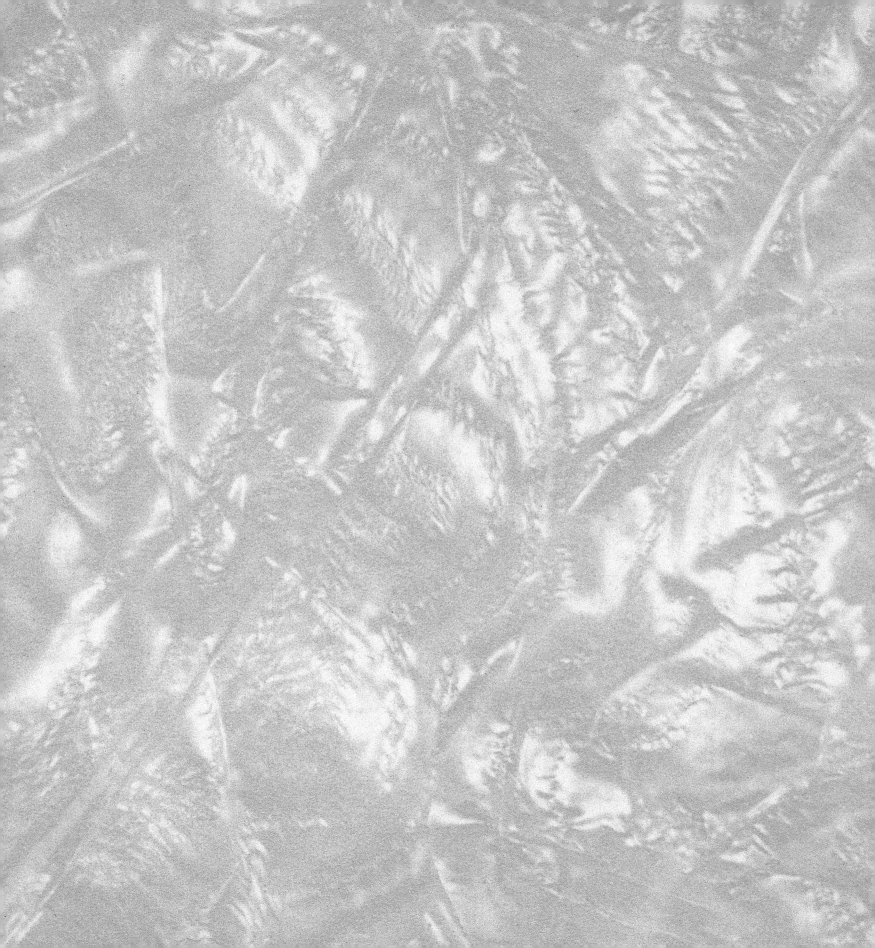

AFTERWORD

The investigation of the future first requires an examination of the past. Formica Corporation has evolved from a typically American grass-roots beginning as an industrial products manufacturer, to a worldwide, design-driven surfacing company which has shaped interiors, design trends, and to a degree, popular culture, for some eighty years.

The global expansion of the company has reached over 150 countries and incorporated as many local cultures, languages, currencies, traditions, and buying preferences in its fold. The bridge to this expansion, the common denominator in a business sense, and the universal language of the global span, has been and will remain design.

The future success of Formica Corporation will come from lessons learned in the past, lessons that were learned the hard way, over many years, and the value of which continues to intellectually elude a surprising number of executives around the world.

In a world of quarterly pressure for profits, of takeovers, junk bonds, and corporate politics, it becomes increasingly difficult for business leaders to understand, or even to take the time to decide to understand, the strategic use of design and the potential competitive advantage to be realized by a design-driven company.

We at Formica Corporation are grateful to the design community, to our own group of design disciples, and to those architects and designers who pushed us and persisted in expanding our conscious corporate capacity to recognize, understand, and clarify the power of design as the foundation of a business strategy.

Our corporate insurance policy for the future is tied directly to our dialogue with the global design community—and our ability to listen and to respond to its needs.

Vincent P. Langone

BIBLIOGRAPHY

A Concise Guide to Plastics.
New York: The Reinhold Publishing Corp., 1960.

Corn, Joseph C., ed.
Imagining Tomorrow: History, Technology, and the American Future.
Cambridge, MA: MIT Press, 1986.

De Long, David G; Helen Searing; and Robert A. M. Stern, eds.
American Architecture: Innovation and Tradition.
New York: Rizzoli International, 1986.

De Wolfe, Elsie.
The House in Good Taste.
Salem, NH: Ayer Company Publishers, 1975.

Armstrong, Richard.
Richard Artschwager.
New York: Whitney Museum in Association with W. W. Norton & Company, Inc., 1988.

Barthes, Roland.
Mythologies.
Translated from the French by Annette Lavers. New York: Hill & Wang, 1972.

Branzi, Andrea.
Learning from Milan.
Cambridge, MA: MIT Press, 1988.

Bush, Donald J.
The Streamlined Decade.
New York: G. Braziller, © 1975.

Drucker, Peter Ferdinand.
Innovation and Entrepreneurship: Practice and Principles.
New York: Harper & Row, © 1985.

DuBois, Harry.
Plastics History U.S.A.
Boston: Cahners, 1972.

Eco, Umberto.
Travels in Hyper Reality.
New York: Harcourt Brace Jovanovich, 1986.

Filler, Martin.
"Surface & Ornament," Surface & Ornament (exhibition catalogue).
Cincinnati: Contemporary Arts Center, 1986.

Forty, Adrian.
Objects of Desire: Design and Society from Wedgwood to IBM.
London: Thames & Hudson Limited, 1986.

Foster, Hal.
Recodings: Art, Spectacle, Cultural Politics.
Port Townsend, WA: Bay Press, 1985.

Freidel, Robert.
Pioneer Plastic: The Making and Selling of Celluloid.
Madison: University of Wisconsin Press, 1983.

Friedan, Betty.
The Feminine Mystique.
New York: W. W. Norton & Company, Inc., 1963.

Glassie, Henry.
Pattern in the Material Folk Culture of the Eastern United States.
Philadelphia: University of Pennsylvania Press, 1969.

Goulden, Joseph C.
The Best Years: 1945–50.
New York: Atheneum, 1976.

Gudis, Catherine, ed.
A Forest of Signs: Art in the Crisis of Representation.
Cambridge, MA: MIT Press, 1990.

Hanks, David A., and Jennifer Toher.
Donald Deskey: Decorative Designs and Interiors.
New York: E. P. Dutton, 1987.

Hayden, Dolores.
Redesigning the American Dream: The Future of Housing, Work, and Family Life.
New York: W. W. Norton & Company, Inc., 1984.

Hess, Alan.
Googie: Fifties Coffee Shop Architecture.
San Francisco: Chronicle Books, 1985.

Hillier, Bevis.
The Style of the Century, 1900–1980.
New York: Dutton, 1983.

Hine, Thomas.
Populuxe.
New York: Alfred A. Knopf, Inc., 1986.

Horn, Richard.
Fifties Style: Then and Now.
New York: Beech Tree Books, © 1985.

Katz, Sylvia.
Plastics: Designs and Materials.
London: Cassell & Collier Macmillan, Ltd., 1978.

Langdon, Philip.
Orange Roofs, Golden Arches: The Architecture of American Chain Restaurants.
New York: Alfred A. Knopf, 1986.

Liebs, Chester.
From Main Street to Miracle Mile.
Boston: Little Brown, 1985.

Luckiesh, Matthew.
Color and Colors.
New York: Van Nostrand Co. Inc., 1938.

Lyotard, Jean-Francois.
The Postmodern Condition: A Report on Knowledge. Translated from the French by Geoff Bennington and Brian Massumi.
Minneapolis: University of Minnesota Press, ©1984.

McLuhan, Marshall, and Quentin Fiore.
The Medium Is the Message.
New York: Random House, 1967.

Material Evidence: New Color Techniques in Handmade Furniture (exhibition catalogue).
Washington, D.C.: Smithsonian Institution, 1985.

Meikle, Jeffrey L.
Twentieth Century Limited: Industrial Design in America, 1925–1939.
Philadelphia: Temple University Press, 1979.

Nelson, George.
George Nelson on Design.
New York: Whitney Library of Design, 1979.

Peters, Thomas J., and Robert H. Waterman, Jr.
In Search of Excellence: Lessons from America's Best-run Companies.
New York: Harper & Row, ©1982.

Politi, Giancarlo, and Helena Kontova, eds.
Flash Art: Two Decades of History.
Cambridge, MA: MIT Press, 1990.

Powell, Polly and Lucy Peel.
'50's & '60's Style.
London: Quintet Publishing Limited, 1988.

Pulos, Arthur J.
American Design Ethic: A History of Industrial Design to 1940.
Cambridge, MA: MIT Press, ©1983.

Radice, Barbara, ed.
Memphis: The New International Style.
Milan: Gruppo Editorale Electa, 1981.

Smith, C. Ray.
Interior Design in 20th-century America: A History.
New York: Harper & Row, 1987.

Smith, Paul J., and Edward Lucie-Smith.
Craft Today: Poetry of the Physical.
American Craft Museum, New York: Weidenfeld & Nicolson, 1986.

Sontag, Susan.
On Photography.
New York: Delta Books/Dell Publishing, 1973.

This Is Tomorrow Today: The Independent Group and British Pop Art (exhibition catalogue, Brian Wallis, curator).
New York: The Institute for Art and Urban Resources, Inc., 1987.

Venturi, Robert.
Complexity and Contradiction in Architecture.
New York: Museum of Modern Art Papers on Architecture, Doubleday & Co., 1966.

Venturi, Robert; Denise Scott Brown; and Steven Izenour.
Learning from Las Vegas.
Cambridge, MA: MIT Press, 1972.

Wright, Gwendolyn.
Building the Dream: A Social History of Housing in America.
Cambridge, MA: MIT Press, 1981.

187

Sarah Bayliss
cocurated the exhibition "Suburban Home Life: Tracking the American Dream" for the Whitney Museum of American Art in 1989. She has written about art for the *Harvard Art Journal* and *Fairfield County Woman.*

Sarah Bodine and Michael Dunas
are writers, lecturers, and curators in the fields of craft, art, and design. They have contributed to *Metropolis, American Ceramics, Metalsmith, Industrial Design,* and *Contemporary Designers* and coauthored *Modern American Jewelry 1940-1970.*

Steven Holt
is a designer and writer. He has been the design director of Zebra Design, Inc., New York, and was the coordinator of product studies at Parsons School of Design. He is a contributing editor and columnist for *Axis* (Japan) and *Metropolitan Home.*

Karrie Jacobs
is a writer-at-large for *Metropolis.* She writes about graphic design, architecture, packaging, and products.

Vincent P. Langone
is the chairman, president, and chief executive officer of Formica Corporation.

Simon Leung
is a lecturer in art criticism for the education department of the New Museum of Contemporary Art in New York.

C O N T R I B U T O R S

Jeffrey L. Meikle
is associate professor of American Studies and Art History at the University of Texas at Austin. He is the author of *Twentieth Century Limited: Industrial Design in America, 1925-1939* and *Design in the Contemporary World.*

Susan Grant Lewin
has been the creative director of Formica Corporation since 1982. She was formerly the senior editor, architecture at *House Beautiful,* and a design editor at Fairchild Publications. Widely recognized for her role as a liaison between industry and the architecture and design communities, she has curated many exhibitions, including "Surface & Ornament," which was exhibited internationally.

R. Craig Miller
is the curator of the department of architecture and design at the Denver Art Museum. He was formerly the associate curator for twentieth-century design at the Metropolitan Museum of Art, New York.

Alessandro De Gregori
is the director of design for Formica Corporation. He was a director of IDSA, the Industrial Designers Society of America, and has taught at the Rhode Island School of Design and Carnegie-Mellon University.

Barbara Goldstein
is project coordinator for the Los Angeles Endowment for the Arts, City of Los Angeles Cultural Affairs Department. She was editor and publisher of *Arts + Architecture* magazine from 1981 to 1985.

Richard J.S. Gutman
is the leading authority on the history and architecture of diners in the United States.

Marybeth Shaw
is currently pursuing a joint master's degree in architecture and urban planning at Massachusetts Institute of Technology, Cambridge, Massachusetts.

FORMICA 33B22

FORMICA #32 DECORATED

FORMICA 278

FORMICA #29 DECORATED

FORMICA #30 DECORATED

FORMICA 10B35

FORMICA K-1114

FORMICA 1B33

INLAYS

FORMICA

SHEET SIZES
WIDTH 24", 30" & 36"
LENGTH 60", 72", 84" & 96"
Furnished in Dull, or in
Polished Finish
Standard or
Cigaretteproof
Grade

FORMICA 54T9

FORMICA 35W29

FORMICA 1008

191